HEALING THE WHOLE PERSON

HEALING THE
WHOLE PERSON

by

GENEVIEVE PARKHURST

MOREHOUSE-BARLOW CO.

NEW YORK

Printed in the United States of America

DEDICATION

This book is affectionately dedicated
to my children

George E. Parkhurst, M.D., his wife Elaine,
and their sons, George Wright and Rodney;

Winifred, her husband, George Wayne Cook,
and their children, Linda, Genevieve, and David;

and to
all who seek wholeness through cooperation with
God's laws, His promises, and His healing love.

ACKNOWLEDGMENTS

The men in my life have helped me keep my thinking straight. My husband, a Christian Clergyman, with his understanding of God's power to heal the soul and spirit, and our son, a Medical Doctor and Psychiatrist, with his knowledge of healing body and mind, have contributed much to my speaking and writing on these kindred subjects.

For some time the question often asked had challenged me. Not, Is divine healing possible? but, How can we touch God for healing? Some day I must try to answer it.

While I was visiting with Miss Edith Leonard and Miss Dorothy VanDeman during the Asilomar Healing Camp near Pacific Grove, California, Miss Leonard handed me a manuscript which contained the story of her healing. I was so thrilled by it that I asked permission to share it with the group assembled that evening. When Edith offered to allow me to use this story I knew it was exactly what I had dreamed of—a detailed account of how one person touched God for healing.

So the book began. It continued with experiences of other friends who told how they had found God's power available for their own needs. Every person whom I asked to share his story seemed glad to write it or to allow me to do so. To each of them I am deeply indebted and wish to express my appreciation for their part in this book.

I thank Edith and Dorothy for reading the manuscript and for polishing some of my faulty phrases. I am indebted to Mr. and Mrs. Arthur Bentley, to Ruth for typing and to Arthur for his helpful comments. Ila Gardner kindly helped with some last minute typing and I thank her.

Here are the authentic stories of many of my friends who have given them in gratitude to God for His goodness to them. It is their hope as well as mine that persons who read them may find courage and faith, even the way to God for their own needs, whether they be physical healing or a closer fellowship with God.

G. P.

FOREWORD

It was my privilege several years ago to share a speakers' platform with Genevieve Parkhurst, who was then unknown to me. Since that time I have traveled around the world, listening to and learning from physicians, psychologists, eminent clergymen and lay figures interested in the healing arts; but none has left a deeper impression on my mind than this serene and unassuming lady.

As daughter and wife of ministers, Mrs. Parkhurst longs to see the modern Church reanimated by the spirit of Christ's own disciples. Her new book is an effort to show something of the human potential that can be awakened by an understanding of His promise, "Lo, I am with you always."

For twenty years before I met Mrs. Parkhurst I had dreamed of bringing together under one roof the arts and skills of medicine, psychology, and religion. In the five years since the vision has become an actuality, we have accumulated impressive evidence that the healing power of the Christ Presence is indeed still operative today and available to all who seek it "in spirit and in faith believing."

Like the protagonist of this book, we are coming to see that Christ's "miracles" are not miracles at all, if by this term is meant the violation of natural law. They are simply a higher application of natural law, a recognition of the spiritual law of God and His universe. For there is a point where mind flows into matter and matter into mind in an endless rhythm. The infinite mind and life of

God are to our mind and life as the ocean is to individual drops of water. No single drop can maintain its existence alone; each is utterly dependent upon the whole ocean, the "living water" of which it is a part.

The unconscious is often symbolized in dreams as an ocean where powers may either overwhelm us or sweep us upward to loftier heights. George Fox described a vision in which he "saw . . . there was an ocean of darkness and death, but an infinite ocean of light and love flowed over the ocean of darkness."

Psychologists once spoke only of the "unconscious" (the ocean of darkness) which harbored all the sunken ships of our guilt-making repressions. But now we find William James, Pitiriam Soroki, Roberto Assagioli, Robert Gerard and others referring to the "superconscious," the ocean of pure and perfect life, the "living waters" whose impingement on our conscious minds brings renewal and healing, not in a miraculous way but in a perfectly natural way.

Once we grasp this fact, we become aware of the immensity of God and understand Christ's prediction, "Greater things than these shall ye do."

As long as we know only the ocean of darkness, we know things only in part; but when we feel the necessity of the presence of God in our lives we begin to sense the ocean of light whose recognition eventually casts out the darkness.

Our own renewing source of physical life is the blood stream. Just as the separation of a pool of water from the parent ocean results in brackishness and eventually evaporation (death), so our failure to maintain conscious contact with the source of life results in its impaired functions. Much research is directed to the study of relation between our food intake and our symptoms; comparatively little to consideration of the "meat which endureth," in the words of Christ.

As physicians, we are ceasing to regard health as merely the absence of symptoms. We are beginning to realize that health means literally wholeness, a balanced expression of physical, mental, emotional, and spiritual elements. This is the "life more abundant."

Through her gentle, but relentless probing for truth, Genevieve Parkhurst leads us on a journey in quest of wholeness. Her authority is Christ Jesus and the Scriptures which give us His words and God's promises of healing. As we become a part of the dramas taken from His life, we feel the pertinency of His teachings for our day as well as for the first century. The authority of Christ's healings for this day is set forth by authentic stories of healings which Mrs. Parkhurst's friends tell in their own words.

For everyone who has asked how it is possible to touch God for healing today, this book can be an absorbing adventure.

Everts G. Loomis, M.D.

Meadowlark Farms
Hemet, California

CONTENTS

HEALING THE WHOLE PERSON

I

HOW CAN WE TOUCH GOD FOR HEALING?

THE MOUNTAIN TRAILS were alluring where aspen whispered among spruce and pines. The air was clean, and water crystal clear from melting snow ran to the valleys from Pikes Peak that shouldered out the sky. Reluctantly I left this natural beauty to go inside a building, even to attend a prayer fellowship. But there I beheld the wonder of God manifest as I had not seen it on the mountain.

During the sharing period Miss Esther, a beautiful young woman whose life is dedicated to teaching children in the public schools, told of having torn cartilage in her knee. She believed God was able to heal it but doctors whom she consulted advised surgery. In order to finish the school term without interruption Esther had walked cautiously, mounting stairs by placing both feet on each step and enduring the pain.

At noon, as the ladies sat around the room eating sack lunches, I felt guided to pray for Esther. Dropping beside her I placed my hands around her knee and held them there a minute or so. First she looked surprised, then her face registered wonder which turned to joy as she realized her knee was healed. All pain and stiffness were gone and there was no restriction in bending. Her knee was perfectly well and has been so ever since.

As easy as that? Yes, but the childlike faith of this young woman was unusual.

What is faith, and what does it mean to believe God, we may ask. Why do persons of childlike faith receive healing when those who try to understand all mysteries do not? Jesus must have given the answer when He said, "Except ye be converted, and become as little children, ye shall not enter into the kingdom of heaven" (Matt. 18:3). What qualities of childhood are so essential to Christian experience that Jesus called them necessary?

Surely one vital quality is the sense of *wonder*. It truly has been said that wonder is the gateway to knowledge. It is equally true that wonder opens the doorway to mystery, awe, and adoration which are at the heart of true worship. Instead of taking for granted things to which we have grown accustomed so that they have become commonplace let us look through the eyes of unspoiled children.

Is it not a miracle to see dry seeds, covered by moist earth, break through the soil and shoot up into green stalks which unfold leaves and branches? As children look at the intricate pattern frost has painted on a window pane or are shown the beauty and symmetry of snowflakes, their faces glow as they ask, "Who made them?" To look at a nest which yesterday contained eggs but today is filled with chirping, downy life is enough to cause childrens' eyes to grow wide in wonder as they ask, "How do eggs turn into chickens?"

The *trust* of a small child might have impressed Jesus. As you look at a baby lying in its mother's arms you see the complete relaxation of his body. He sleeps with no thought of harm, no feeling of fear, but in absolute confidence in the arms that hold him. Watch a child who is hurt run to his mother for solace and comfort. Her arm around him is security, her smile is light, and her kiss makes the hurt place better. Friends are acceptable when all is well but, when trouble comes, no one can take the place of his mother. He feels secure in her presence.

Belief is a third childlike characteristic valuable to Christians. An innocent child accepts all that is told him as truth. With starry-eyed confidence he looks into the faces of his parents, believing every word they say. If the parents are honest, the child develops respect for truth.

Jesus saw characteristics of the child which enrich life in the home and likened them to the Christian's attitude toward God. The Creator, whose greatness overwhelms us as we contemplate His creation, becomes Our Father who understands and loves us. In Him is our security. We may recall His words, "As one whom his mother comforteth; so will I comfort you" (Is. 66:13). As the child secure in his home life is able to go into the world and face difficulties, so the Christian should be able to endure hardships through the power of God who upholds him. He who has grown up with the knowledge of truth should be able to discern error in later life.

In this triad of childhood virtues, wonder says, "Of course there is a God." Trust says, "God made me, loves me and I can rely on Him." Belief affirms God's promises as true, irrefutable, unchanging, and stands on them, undaunted.

The Eternal God does not change but is the same yesterday, today and forever. Man's belief in Him sets the boundaries which determine how far God shall come into his life. God's power begins exactly where man's faith takes hold.

To those who think of God as a benevolent influence such as sunshine, everywhere present but impersonal, He is that to them. Still they may be helped by taking themselves into the warmth of divine love and basking there, as they may be benefitted by bathing in sunshine.

Persons who recognize that all healing is of God, since all life comes from Him, should be able to become receptive to this healing within as they allow the Divine Life to work through the cells of the body, restoring and rebuilding.

Just as we ask a blessing on our food at table, so we should pray God to bless our medicine as we take it. As our bodies adjust to health we may feel that medicine is no longer necessary. Only reputable doctors are able to tell persons what they should take and when to take it. To stop taking such medicine as insulin might be disastrous.

In reliance on doctors and hospital care for healing, we should pray for all who care for us. Many physicians say there is no disagreement between intelligent prayer and the wise practice of medicine. The effectiveness of prayer often has been demonstrated during surgical operations when doctors, nurses, and patient were undergirded by the prayer's of someone or many while surgery was in progress. Surgeons have spoken to me of times when everyone in the operating theater was at his and her best, alert and cooperative, when every instrument they touched was the right one, and every move furthered the work to satisfactory completion.

God's healing is not a thing apart from life, but is one with the spirit that is our real selves. From the Creator comes the total life of man. It is He who created our bodies, endowed us with intelligence, and gave life to our individual spirits. All the methods we have spoken of are good as they help us to bring ourselves into co-operation with the life of God, yet Christ shows us a way which is above all material methods.

Saint Paul wrote to the Corinthian Church concerning the gifts of the Spirit. After he had gone into detail as to the value and use of these marvelous gifts, which the Holy Spirit had given the early Church to empower them to witness for Christ, Paul concludes his dissertation by saying, "But covet earnestly the best gifts: and yet shew I unto you a more excellent way" (I Cor. 12:31). He then unfolded to them the way of love, which has been recorded in the thirteenth chapter of First Corinthians. Above and beyond every good and perfect gift, he is saying, is that which is supreme, and it is love. Use the gifts, yes, but strive to attain to the highest.

Christ's healing is *the more excellent way.* Use all wisdom to maintain health; seek the service of the best doctors when you must; but in your heart know there is the *more excellent way,* and it is for you. Know it because you know God. You have experienced the transforming power of His presence as you committed your life to Him. At times you have felt His Spirit moving in your heart, lifting you to heights above mortal thought.

Healings were a great part of Jesus' ministry. Before He left His disciples He commissioned them to go into all the world and preach the gospel, to heal the sick and cast out demons. This work is ours, for He said, "Neither pray I for these alone, but for them also which shall believe on me through their word." (Jn. 17:20). After Jesus left them, the disciples' power to heal was so great that sick persons were carried into the streets and laid on beds and couches "that at least the shadow of Peter passing by might over-shadow some of them" (Acts 5:15).

So empowering was the Holy Spirit which filled the early

Christians that they wavered not as they endured persecution, hid in Catacombs, were fed to lions, and burned at the stake. Their steadfast loyalty to Christ upheld them for more than two centuries, even until the proud Roman Empire was brought to her knees.

When Christians lost the power of the Spirit and turned to ways of the world, their strength waned. There followed inquisitions and persecutions until, little by little, reliance on God faded away. So little faith remained in the Church that the Sacrament of Christ's body and blood became the last rites for the dying, and any manifestation of God's power was considered a miracle. The Dark Ages followed when the light of faith was kept burning by holy men who hid away in monasteries.

But "the darkness can not put out the Light." Never, since the time of Christ, has it been extinguished. There have been times of decline followed by times of revival when new leaders arose, filled with inspiration. So the tides of religious fervor have lifted and fallen.

Certain barometers have indicated the height of the tide. When the Light has flickered low in the Church the certainty of Christ's presence has become vague. Forms and rituals have remained, but the transforming power of God has no longer been in evidence. The ministry of healing has usually been the first rite to be discontinued.

When man's intellect and ingenuity are esteemed more highly than the Eternal God, when people listen approvingly to such blasphemous chants as that "God is dead," the trough in the wave of eternal truth is of cavernous proportions. It will swallow us unless there is a lift of the tide.

But the tide is coming in! God's power is again moving among us. It is being manifest in true and ancient forms. Healings are once again taking place quietly in many sacred places.

Persons who are humble seem to receive God's blessings more readily than persons of strong personal opinions and great self-esteem. Perhaps the ego, the self, becomes enthroned in such persons and it is impossible for God to break through this barrier.

The master of a southern mansion lay moaning in his bed. His wife and I stood beside him. I was praying silently, for I desired to help this man whose family had asked me to visit. I spoke to him of God's love and Jesus' healing power but he only rolled his head and groaned. There was no question that he heard me, for he had talked of other things before I mentioned the subject of prayer. Evidently his mind was closed to this possibility. At his wife's request I offered a prayer, and we left the room.

She went into the kitchen while I stood beside the dining room windows, looking out at the garden. I was thinking of Naaman, a man of importance who became angry and felt himself humiliated because the prophet Elisha directed him to do such an undignified thing as to dip himself seven times in the river Jordan, after he had traveled to see him, seeking healing for his leprosy. Surely the prophet should have recognized his station in life and have asked him to do something fitting his dignity. In his anger Naaman turned away.

"How beautifully your gardener keeps your flowers," I said as the lady of the house joined me.

"Yes, he is a good gardener," she answered, "but he is not well. He has very bad heart trouble."

"Would he allow me to pray for him?" I asked quickly.

"Oh, would you?" the question was an exclamation.

Together we went outside where she explained to the old Negro who was working there, who I was and why I had come; then she left us.

Looking to the far end of the garden I saw an old chair leaning against a tree, and suggested we go to it. As we walked, I explained to this humble man, who followed close behind me, that God loves us so much He is happy to give us His grace for our physical healing. When we reached the chair I suggested he sit down. He stood looking at the ground, twisting his hat in his hands. Finally he muttered, 'Mam, I can't sit in yo' presence, you standin'."

I had to swallow hard before I could speak. Then I explained to him that we both were in the presence of our heavenly Father and suggested we revere Him. He sat in the chair and I placed one hand on his chest, the other on his back, and prayed that God would heal his heart. It seemed that angels gathered around us, for the light of God flooded us until I was filled with joy. The face of this humble servant was aglow with a light not of this world as his heart overflowed with gratitude for the healing he felt within himself.

This experience turns my thoughts to another which reveals the power of looking to God until one is lost in adoration.

Mrs. Shultz had the misfortune to spill boiling oil on her left hand. The burn was deep, the pain intense. After it was treated, she returned home and found the sedative given her did not dull the pain. She walked the floor for awhile, then slipped out and went to her church.

Kneeling at the chancel, she looked up at the picture of Jesus in the stained glass window above the altar. As she lifted her thoughts in adoration of Him, she lost all consciousness of pain, of her body and her surroundings. As she looked intently at the figure in the window it seemed to glow. Christ was real to her. Nothing existed at this hour but God, His wonder and His love.

As Mrs. Schultz left the church, she noticed there was no pain in her hand. Later, when the bandages were removed, new pink skin covered the area where the burns had been. Amazed, she wondered how such a miracle had happened to her.

God does not break His laws. Healings which result from prayer follow the same recuperative process as normal healings, but usually the time required for their completion is greatly accelerated. God is not bound by time as we are. God can collapse time for "with the Lord one day is as a thousand years." (II Pet. 3:8, RSV). This can explain the rapid healing of a burn or the disappearance of a tumor.

"The spirit of man is the candle of the Lord," says Proverbs 20:27. As we worship Him, we allow His light to illumine our beings. When we come to Him for healing, we lift the candle of our spirits up to Him until contact is made and the smoldering spark in the citadel of our souls bursts into flame. This light brings our bodies into harmony with His spirit so that we may experience wholeness.

Seemingly solid substances are largely gases and vibrations. Visible things are but a fraction of the invisible universe about us. Is there a better explanation of what takes place when a burn is instantly healed or a tumor dissolves into nothingness than to remember that God is all and in all?

Man's knowledge of material laws has far outrun his knowledge of the Spirit, for his interest has been focused largely on material progress. Science has made many advances in the realm of the invisibles, yet knowledge of the Spirit, which is the greatest of all invisibles, has remained underdeveloped. This may be true because man must submit himself to the Teacher if he is to learn well. Man is not often interested in submitting himself humbly since it has been his privilege to do as he pleased with the free will God has given him.

Still, we are able to use some things without knowing all about them. We do not know what electricity is, but we use it in many ways to serve us. We also can channel the power of God's Spirit to meet human needs. Jesus likened the Holy Spirit to the wind, and as we know when a gale is blowing, we know when the Spirit renews life in a human soul or body.

Mrs. Mittie Waters who visits many Southern prisons as a friend, the prisoner's "other mother" and spiritual counselor, says there is a spark of the divine light in the sacred sanctuary of every soul. She often has seen the so-called "worst criminals" among both men and women prisoners respond to kindness. When expressed through human kindness "the goodness of God leadeth to repentance." The warmth of love melts icy barriers and the divine spark within, which has been repressed, and smothered, is fanned into flame in the citadel of the inmost being. It is love that brings God's light to flame in the human heart.

Mittie Waters is so filled with divine love that she gives of herself to the poor unfortunates in prisons as a loving mother gives to her children. A service of such unselfish devotion is a witness to God's power and grace.

A sadness comes over me as I think of these prisoners, and I feel that there, but for the Grace of God, go I. The unfortunate ones condemned to prison have committed acts while in the heat of anger or passion, or have grown up lacking the warmth of love and Christian training which has been ours. We who walk free, our heads high, have been able to repress our anger, conceal our hates and jealousies, hide our mean attitudes, so that they have not broken out in acts which reveal the dark side of our natures. We are respectable.

But, "the Lord seeth not as man seeth; for man looketh on the outward appearance, but the Lord looketh on the heart" (I Sam. 16:7). What does God see as He looks through us? As we come to God for His healing grace, it is necessary that we cleanse our hearts by confessing all sins of attitudes, omissions, and unforgiven faults. If His Spirit brings things to our minds that should be made right, we must be willing to make the effort to correct them.

Our hearts cannot be cleansed until we have forgiven everyone who has hurt us in any way or against whom we hold resentment. Jesus emphasized the necessity of forgiving all who trespass against us, even forgiving as God forgives us. We may pray, "Create in me a clean heart, O God; and renew a right spirit within me" (Ps. 51:10).

When approaching God for His blessings let us obey His commandment, "Therefore if thou bring thy gift to the altar, and there rememberest that thy brother hath ought against thee; Leave there thy gift before the altar, and go thy way; first be reconciled to thy brother, and then come and offer thy gift" (Matt. 5:23, 24).

Many persons receive healing when they recognize the wisdom of God as superior to their own, submit their wills to His and, lifting their faith, release it as one might give a captive bird to the sky. There is a spark of the Divine in each of us that yearns for freedom. The freedom we yearn for may be the life God has for us.

Nothing is more helpful in receiving healing than an unshaken belief in God's power. Children's faith often puts

us who have grown worldly-wise to shame. When asked who
would enter the Kingdom of God, Jesus set a child in the
midst of His questioners and answered, ". . . of such is the
kingdom of God" (*cf*. Mk. 10:13-16; Lk. 18:15-17).

Lawrence expressed such unquestioning faith. He smiled
happily as I approached his bed. After we had talked
together for some minutes, I asked, "Larry, do you believe
God can heal you?"

Looking up at me with large brown eyes, the boy said
with utter candor, "Why, God can do anything."

With Larry's belief in God's power to "do anything," I
could pray with confidence that even so serious a condition
as his would be healed. And it was.

Certainly God *can* do anything. But there are things God
does not do without the consent of the will of man. Having
given man free will, God respects man's right to make
choices. God is a perfect gentleman. He never pushes in
where He is not invited, neither does he coerce any person.
If we want God in our lives we must ask Him to come in.

God is both transcendent and immanent. He is beyond
us, yet He is in us. His greatness empowers human limitations when man's life is in accord with His will. Yet, God
in all his greatness can do no more in the lives of indi-
viduals than they will allow Him to do.

Talking with me about Christian healing, a young medic
said sarcastically, "If God can heal through you, why don't
you go to the hospital and heal everybody there—empty
the hospital! Heal every person as you walk through!"

I looked at him a moment, then asked, "Why doesn't
your father, who is a Christian Clergyman, go to the con-

gested areas of large cities and transform all the thugs, the dope addicts, the drunkards, thieves, rapists, murderers, all the wicked, conniving criminals who are there and change them into Christian characters as he walks through their midst?"

"Don't be absurd," the young man countered, but the twinkle in his eyes as he smiled showed that he saw the parallel.

As we turn from cynicism and self-importance and look away from the sordidness of destruction about us, let us no longer feel we must analyze and evaluate everything according to human wisdom. Rather, let us try to contemplate the reality which witnesses to the deep things of human experience. So doing, we may be lifted out of the groove of dull routine and once more have the capacity of wonder, of trust, and belief in a power greater than our own.

In our effort to understand how God's power is effective through prayer let us relinquish our little wisdom to the Ocean of All-Knowing. Here we lose ourselves to find our greater lives as a drop of water becomes one with the ocean. In this way we experience "losing our lives," as Jesus said we must if we are to find life more abundant in Him. So giving ourselves and merging into the Divine, God is able to stamp His likeness upon us.

II

FIND A LEVER AND MOVE YOUR MOUNTAINS

O RDINARILY LEVERS are used to move objects too heavy to be lifted by hand. By placing a strong timber beneath the thing to be moved, resting it on a firm fulcrum, and applying downward pressure to the loose end, great force is exerted. The use of the lever is not new. The Greek mathematician, Archimedes, said centuries ago, "Give me a lever long enough and a fulcrum strong enough and I can move the earth."

Spiritual levers are useful in moving obstacles to our faith. We depend so much on our physical senses that it is helpful to find something we can see, feel, and touch to use as a lever to clear away the doubts that obstruct our vision of God's availability for our needs.

In His marvelous wisdom, Jesus spoke divine truths but He clothed them in illustrations so simple that even the unlearned could understand what He was saying. He expressed infinite wisdom in finite terms. His parables were levers that people could grasp with their understanding. Many who listened to Him had engaged in the activities recounted in the stories He told. As they listened they identified themselves with the persons whom Jesus made real to them.

There are levers we can use. Let us think of some of these.

Spiritual levers enable us to move mountains of difficulties. We have confidence to do this when we know who we are and whose we are. When we realize we are God's children, created by Him, loved of Him, and surrounded by His constant care, we are fortified by a sense of importance. Such consciousness makes us realize our worth. This understanding enables us to stand straight, look the world in the face, and go forward in the strength of Him whose we are.

Great promises are given those who abide in Him. To abide is to live permanently and make one's home in a place. Abiding in Christ we synchonize our lives with His. So we can use great affirmations and say with fervor,

I belong to Christ, I belong to Christ, I belong to Christ.
Christ is my way, my truth and my life;
In Him I live and move and have my being;
Christ is my peace, my power, my plenty.
I belong to Christ, I belong to Christ, I belong to Christ.

Affirm this until, as Jesus said, you are "hid with Christ in God." When you experience this oneness with Him, you can forget yourself as you give your interest to others. There is great joy in doing this.

Persons have been healed as they looked away from their own needs and prayed for others. Jesus showed such great compassion for all people in need that we may become like Him when we are filled with compassion for others. I saw a woman's hands, gnarled and stiff from arthritis, become flexible after she had been in earnest prayer for a boy who was in critical condition. Filled with joy and surprise, she later said, "Why did God heal me? I did not ask Him to. That dear boy was in much greater need than I was. God has been so good to me I could not ask Him for anything for myself."

Through relinquishment we find a marvelous power in prayer. When we come to God and release our burdens, of whatever kind they may be—sins, hurts, responsibility for others, even our sicknesses—and give them completely to Him as Jesus gave to God the evils that were heaped upon Him, and went forth calmly to finish the course set before Him, so we may know such release and peace, even our healing. Relinquishment seems to be the most difficult part of prayer. Yet it is surely most important. Until we give our concerns to God and turn loose of them He is not able to channel transforming power to us. It has been well said that praying and yet holding to our anxieties is like trying to water flowers while we have our foot on the garden hose.

When praying for persons who are ill, do not think of them as sick, but visualize them as being completely well. There is no sickness in heaven, nor is there any sickness in God. When holding our friends in God's love, lift them to the highest.

Never feel you must tell God the gory details of an illness or accident. He knows them already and telling them stamps the unpleasant condition on your mind and binds them to the person you long to release. What did Jesus mean when he said, "Whatever you bind on earth shall be bound in heaven, and whatever you loose on earth shall be loosed in heaven" (Matt. 16:19, RSV)? Jesus was speaking to Peter, but do we not also have power to bind and to loose persons by our attitudes? "Keep [guard] thy heart

with all diligence; for out of it are the issues of life"
(Prov. 4:23).

When we are able to identify ourselves with persons
Jesus healed we then have a powerful lever for our own
healing. Often it helps to make some physical contact
which will enable our faith to be lifted.

Mrs. Godfrey had prayed for healing but had seen no
change in her physical condition. One day as she stood in
the sanctuary of her church, looking at a stained glass
window which portrayed Jesus standing outside a closed
door, she remembered the story of the woman who touched
the hem of His garment and was healed. In reverent worship her thoughts lifted in adoration. A deep yearning
filled her as she longed to touch Jesus. In this attitude she
lifted her hand and let the tips of her fingers rest on the
hem of His garment, as the sun shone through the glass.
When she did this, a vibration like electricity went through
her body and she felt the joy of complete healing. This
healing was later confirmed by her doctor.

Persons have been healed as they touched their television
screen or cabinet while a powerful healing presentation was
being broadcast. The television afforded a visible lever for
the beholder and healing came through the faith of the
individual who watched and believed.

There is wonderful power in visualizing the good we
desire and in holding a picture of this desired well-being
firmly in our minds. It is possible to hold in mind that
which we desire until our mental power applied to the lever
of believing helps to bring into actuality that which fervently is longed for.

Henry was so crippled in an automobile accident that little hope was given that he ever would be able to walk again. But Henry was determined to walk and run as he once had. He asked that a clip board be placed by his bed, and on it he tacked pictures of athletes running, jumping, playing tennis, swimming, and in various other activities. Many hours Henry lay quietly looking at the pictures of these boy's strong bodies, and saying to himself, as he flexed the muscles in his seemingly lifeless legs, "I will run again! I will! I will!" Then, as if speaking to some invisible adversary, he would nod his head and say, "You'll see!" Henry did walk again. He also ran on a track team and made good time. Who can say how much the boy's steadfast determination enabled him to attain his goal?

One day the mother of a high school boy opened her door to the school athletic coach who told her that her son had been badly burned in an explosion in the chemistry laboratory. He had been taken to the local hospital where she might go to see him.

This mother believed in prayer and knew the power of visualizing good. When she saw her son he was swathed in bandages. She spoke to him encouragingly, then went home to "see her son perfect," as she said. She sat before a table on which she had placed pictures of this boy in track trunks. Looking at these pictures, she affirmed over and over again, "This is my son, his body is strong and whole." Several times a day this mother repeated these affirmations. Closing her eyes she created on the screen of her mind the picture of her son's body, perfectly whole. Steadfastly she held to Jesus' promise, ". . . whatever you ask in prayer, believe that you receive it, and you will" (Mk. 11:24, RSV).

The recovery of this youth was phenomenal. Although doctors who attended him expected considerable skin grafting would be necessary, none was needed. The boy was able to leave the hospital sooner than was expected and, happily, no scars remained after a few weeks.

Think of yourself as a healthy person and of your general well-being as good. Regard feelings of illness as temporal and realize that such are to be expected as a result of overwork mental strain, and staying too long at any task without sufficient periods of relaxation. Of course if illness grows worse, it is wise to consult your physician; and symptoms which point to a malignant growth should have immediate attention. Pray, but do all you can to maintain health.

Medical Doctors do not expect to contract the diseases of the patients whom they treat. Their work is to cure diseases and enable their patients to get well. Their thought is on healing. With this attitude they are able to go from one sick room to another, giving encouragement, administering medications, and keeping themselves well as they do so.

When we expect sickness, we draw it to us. The influence of fear of sickness and anticipating illness is forcefully stated by Edward Von Herman in his book *The Philosophy of the Unconscious:* [1] "The surest way to be taken with an infectious disease is to be afraid of it . . . . Lively fear and the thought of sickness is of itself sufficient to cause the same without any infection, especially if it is heightened by the terror of incurring risk."

God has endowed each of us with a degree of common sense. Let us use it. When we drive ourselves beyond en-

---

[1] W. B. Saunders Co., Philadelphia.

durance, we must pay for the nerve strain our bodies have endured. This usually requires more rest than is normally necessary for us. I truly must repent before I can ask God to heal me of that which I have brought onto myself. When I realize I am working beyond the point of endurance, I know that later I must rest until my body restores its balance. Many illnesses are the result of insufficient rest. Work follows work, stress is heaped upon stress, until some part of the body mechanism breaks down and demands, in sickness, the opportunity to rebuild its overworked nerves and tissues. When we reach the place we feel unable to rest without the aid of sleeping pills, we should heed the warning signal and stop before we go headlong into serious physical or mental trouble.

It is wise to rest before a period of strain, rather than after it. A college professor who usually came down with a spell of grippe or "flu" after the semester's examinations wisely decided to rest before they began. Testing his theory, he went to bed as soon as he reached home on the Friday before the examinations began, and stayed there until Sunday afternoon. He rested, dozed, read, and listened to his favorite records, as he stretched out between the sheets. He was not at home to visitors and the telephone. To his relief, he went through the closing days of the school term happily.

We should allow our bodies time to heal. It was said of some whom Jesus healed that from the hour He touched them, they began to mend. The ten lepers who came to Him were healed as they went on their way.

As Christians, we know that, "in him we live, and move, and have our being"; so we should trust His power to refresh and renew us.

The most powerful lever that can be used for attaining healing is the Word of God in the Bible. We can read books, talk with people, seek the help of persons who are reputed to have power in healing, yes, we can even pray; but when we want the power of God, we should turn to His promises. Although God is invisible, the results of obeying His Words have visible rewards. In the Bible we find words of instruction, counsel, advice, and encouragement. These words also contain promises which are fulfilled to us when we meet the prescribed conditions. There is a promise to meet every need.

God led the children of Israel into a Promised Land. He has prepared for us a Land of Promises. When the Israelites went to possess the land which was promised them, they had to go into it and claim every portion of it as they put their feet upon it and withstood the enemy. If we are to possess God's promises, we must stand upon them in spite of winds of doubt that blow and trials that threaten to overwhelm us.

It is surprising that many people know practically nothing of the promises in the Bible. Often when a person comes to me asking for prayer, I ask him, what promise in the Bible he is relying on. Sometimes a blank look comes over his face and he says, "The Lord is my shepherd; I shall not want." If I ask for a more specific promise, he cannot quote another verse.

We cannot expect to enter into the blessings God has for us unless we know what He inspired consecrated men to write. While the simplicity of a child-like trust in God is commendable, He also led St. Paul to say, "Study to shew thyself approved unto God, a workman that needeth not to be ashamed, rightly dividing [interpreting] the word of truth" (II Tim. 2:15). If we want God's approval, we must "search the scriptures." The blueprint for building a life is outlined in God's Word.

If some relative were to leave you a large sum of money in his will you would exert every effort to possess it. Your Heavenly Father has bequeathed to you great spiritual riches. His will for you is written in His Word. Find it— your heritage. You are His child. Study to claim what is rightfully yours.

Make a notebook of God's promises as you find them in the Bible. Claim each one as especially your own. It will help in your study if you will mark your Bible with colored pencils. A well-marked Bible gives an invitation to read. You might underline every promise with blue; every reference to health, long life, and healing with red; and the verses that have reference to praise and thanksgiving, with yellow. If you do this, the blue of the summer sky will smile at you as you open your Bible; the red, rich as the blood of Christ, will speak to you of life; and the Psalms will glow like a field of daffodils.

Set aside some time every day for study and worship. It is best if the same hour is used each day. Begin by getting quiet and asking God to enlighten your mind and speak to you. Read a chapter from the Gospels. Each writer is interesting for he tells of Jesus' teachings and actions. Read consecutively so that your reading will have continuity. Then read a psalm. Begin with Psalms 1, 8, 15, 19, 23, 19, 37, 103, and 139.

Meditate on God's goodness; then talk to Him aloud. Voice your prayers. Say what is in your heart. Be honest. Lay all pretense aside. Surely God is more pleased with honesty spoken in slang than in precise language of deceit. One of the best prayers I ever heard was given by a young man in a Youth Camp. When he was called on to pray he was silent a moment, then blurted out, "God, I'm mad. I'm mad about this situation that all of us know about, and You know more about it than any of us do. Give us the guts to do the right thing. Amen."

That was an honest prayer. Surely God was delighted with it. The fellow who prayed it meant business. God must get tired of the pious mutterings of people who pretend to be what they are not. Not only does God have a sense of humor but He must delight in spontaneous expression of truth.

When you know God's promises, act upon them. Most people want to see perfect results before they believe their prayers are answered. They place their trust in evidence visible to the eye rather than on God's promise. Faith believes without seeing. If you are sure your prayer is within the will of God (after all, we pray in the Lord's Prayer, "Thy will be done on earth as it is in heaven"), when your request hurts no one but benefits you and others, and its answer will further God's kingdom on earth, you have a right to ask it. Furthermore, you have a right to believe God is working out the answer even before you see the evidence of it.

Reverend Kenneth E. Hagin of Tulsa, Oklahoma, tells a remarkable story of his own healing. When in his latter teens he was stricken with facial paralysis which left one side of his face numb, his left eyelid unmovable and his mouth drawn. Such a condition was distressing to a young man conscious of his appearance.

But Kenneth believed the Bible was God's Word and that the promises of Jesus meant exactly what they said. He read in James 5 (Verses 14-15), "Is any sick among you? let him call for the elders of the church; and let them pray over him; anointing him with oil in the name of the Lord: And the prayer of faith shall save the sick, and the Lord shall raise him up; and if he have committed sins, they shall be forgiven him."

Kenneth accepted these words as truth and acted upon them. At the close of a church service he asked his pastor to pray for his healing. This was done but after the service of prayer and anointing no change was evidenced in the young man's appearance.

Undaunted, Kenneth walked with his girl friend to her home. When they entered the house the young lady said to her mother, "Kenneth thought he was healed tonight when Brother Carter prayed for him."

"I did not think I was healed. I know it," Kenneth spoke up.

"Why, your face looks just like it did," the girl protested.

"It does not matter what my face looks like, I was healed," Kenneth affirmed.

"How can you say a thing like that when your mouth pulls over to your ear every time you smile?" the girl questioned.

"The healing isn't manifested yet, but it is done," the boy declared.

"How do you know?" the girl persisted.

"I know because God's Word says so. God cannot lie. Whatever He says in the Bible is true." Kenneth held his ground.

"Maybe Kenneth knows something about faith that we don't know," the mother said to her daughter. "Let's wait and see what the result it."

With approval of the mother's understanding, Kenneth spoke up, "I know that God is eternal truth and that His

Word never fails. His promise is that if anyone is sick to call the elders of the church and let them pray for him, anointing him in the name of the Lord, and the prayer of faith shall heal the sick. I did what the Word said to do; Brother Carter did what the word said to do; now it is up to God to do what He says He will do."

With this assertion, the young man went home and to bed. As he lay in darkness, occasionally noting the time on the luminous dial of the clock on his bedside table, he began to thank God for the healing that was to be manifest in His own good time. He continued to thank God for fifteen minutes, a half hour, forty minutes, before he dropped off to sleep. The next morning when he looked in the mirror, behold! his face was normal, perfectly healed.

Reverend Mr. Hagin said: "Perhaps God delays His healing at times to test our faith and see if we really believe Him." It may be that many are not healed because they can not stand such a test.

What can we say in the light of such an experience? Here was a faith that rose to knowing, and gratitude that was expressed in thanksgiving, even before the desired healing was manifest.

III

REJOICE, YOU ARE GOD'S CHILD

THERE ARE PERSONS who feel they are not good enough for God to heal them. Some think themselves unworthy of God's love. Such an attitude may be the result of treatment they received when they were children. If parents make a child feel inferior, he may have this same feeling as he thinks of God.

When such a person receives a healing through prayer, he scarcely can believe such a thing has happened to him. He may agree that God might heal others, but he is not worthy of such a miracle. He may say, "this is too good to be true." Saying this, he really is saying it is not true, although he longs for it to be a reality. Unbelieving and refusing to accept the healing, he loses it, and grieves that God does not love him enough to heal him.

Beloved, take heart. You are a child of God, precious in His sight. If you have strayed from His care, return to His fellowship, knowing He waits for you with open arms. If you truly are a Christian, you are an heir of God, a joint heir with His Son Jesus Christ. God's love surrounds and blesses you as you recognize it.

All of God's children are entitled to share in His riches. Jesus made this clear in His story of the Prodigal Son. In this drama God is portrayed by the father, persons who repent and return to the Father's house are represented by the Prodigal Son, and nominal Christians who feel no need of repentance and experience no close fellowship with the Father are seen in the role of the Elder Brother.

As the drama reaches its climax and the feast of the fatted calf is being eaten in rejoicing that the erring son has returned home, the Elder Brother sulks outside, complaining that his father never gave him a kid that he might make merry with friends. Seeing this, the Father says to him, "Son, all that I have is yours."

Not realizing the heritage that was his, the Elder Brother asked for nothing. He might have had a feast with his friends at any time, but he did not. He must have worked without enjoyment and have felt poor because he thought himself poor. The most crushing poverty is not lack of money but the poverty of mind that cripples the initiative, cowers and degrades the personality. Many have been without funds, but have been rich in friends and empowered by the hope of better days. Our Father's riches are measureless, but we seldom receive more than we realize belongs to us, or than we ask for, accept, and give thanks for.

As in many areas of life, our attitude of mind determines our wealth of spiritual grace. There is great truth in the ancient words, "As a man thinketh in his heart, so is he." The heart here referred to might be called the subconscious mind today. If we knew more about this deep area of our being, we would understand ourselves better. Leaving the psychological language to trained psychologists, we might think of the complexity of our minds as I have explained it to children.

Let us say that the conscious mind is the Man who lives on the Ground Floor of our House of Life. He is the person in us who thinks, reasons, wills, plans, and determines what he will do. He enjoys fellowship with other people, has various experiences, and, trusting his intelligence, thinks he is master of the house. To keep his living room presentable for reception of guests, he opens the basement door and pushes all unsightly clutter into the room below.

The Man's Partner, his subconscious, who lives in the basement, takes all that is given him and files it away. He can draw out the memory of every thought, act, and experience of the Man on the Ground Floor and remind him of it at any time. In this way he can hinder the Man, as he makes him fear new ventures because of past experiences.

Man's Partner is primitive, unable to reason, and is motivated by instincts and emotions, especially those of self-preservation and sex. He cannot reason, but acts from feelings. He is slow to think, but when his mind is made up it is not easily changed. This Partner, like a building maintenance engineer, cares for the functioning of the organs of the human body. Centuries before the Man on the Ground Floor acquired the veneer of civilization, his Partner was in charge of the body-house.

This Partner is a powerful ally when he is in harmony with the Man on the Ground Floor; when in agreement, they tend to create a strong character. The Man gives orders to his Partner, who carries them out. If the Man sneezes and says, "I think I am taking a cold," his Partner, who issues orders to every cell in the body, tells them, "Produce a cold. We have an order for it." So, the Man has a cold. Slow to accept change, the Partner may refuse to believe what the Man tells him, especially if it is a new idea. The Man may see the reasonableness of God's power to heal, but his Partner, being stubborn, may deny this and mutter, "It is not so. I don't believe it." And the Man is not healed.

The Partner's attitudes can be changed by repeatedly sending down to him the ideas which the Man wishes him to act upon. When only truthful, optimistic, and hopeful words are spoken, the Partner will finally accept and act upon them. Here is the value of positive thinking and happy anticipation, for we become what our thinking is.

Another area of the mind, the superego, might be called the Cherub in the Penthouse. Here is our conscience, and through him come our aspiration and inspiration. The Cherub forms his ideas of right and wrong from the attitudes and actions of the Man on the Ground Floor. While he is receptive to inspiration from God, he, like the Partner in the Basement, must accept that which the Man, who is boss of the House of Life, tells him.

It is possible for the Cherub to be denied repeatedly, made to feel unworthy and ashamed until he cowers and is no longer able to make his voice heard by the Man who wields authority over him.

This Cherub in the Penthouse of our lives is like the child whom Jesus said represented those who would enter the kingdom of heaven. Since God is love, love is necessary for the growth of the Cherub in the Penthouse of our lives. Persons who have been deeply hurt during childhood usually carry a weight of guilt, most of it imagined because they have been told they were no good, could do nothing right, were clumsy, or never would amount to anything. Denied the love and approval of parents and persons around them, they question that even God can love them.

In later life, such persons may not be able to associate freely with others, so they become withdrawn, passive, and may be called "loners." Others who are more aggressive may retaliate against society and become outlaws; they grow belligerent and hard as they refuse all efforts to help them.

When every area of an individual's mind is in harmonious relationship, his personality is a unified whole. This makes for strength of character which cannot be experienced if one area of the mind is pulling against another. Such division weakens an individual's efforts so that he may be likened to the "double minded man" to whom James referred (Jas. 1:6-8) as being "unstable in all his ways." James also wrote ". . . let not that man think that he shall receive any thing of the Lord." That man, says James, is as unstable as "a wave of the sea."

When the whole mind is in harmonious relationship, the personality may be likened to the hind, or female deer, which is the most sure-footed of all animals. When bounding up mountain crags she sets her rear feet in the exact tracks her forefeet have made. Seeing where her front feet are placed, she knows her back feet will not slip. So she mounts up safely and surely. David must have known this centuries ago, for in Psalm 18, verse 33, he wrote, concerning God's guidance, "He maketh my feet like hinds' feet, and setteth me upon my high places."

When there is oneness of mind, life is not departmentalized as if no relationship exists between spirit, mind, and body. Each area enriches the whole, each imparting, receiving, and sustaining the entire being. Divine healing becomes real when the mind sanctions it, the spirit accepts it, and the body manifests it.

Oh, dear reader, whoever you are, wherever you are and whatever experiences you have endured, lift up your hearts and allow the love of your Father, God, to come into your life. Allow Him to heal your memories, to give you the assurance of sins forgiven, to touch your body, and fill you with the joy of His abiding love.

You are God's child, created in His image. Into you He breathed the breath of life. If you have strayed from His care, return to Him. Allow His love to surround you, assuring, sustaining, and giving you courage. It may be that you have been hurt, and, because of this, you have not realized the potentials God gave you, nor attained the fullness of life He has for you.

In Ephesians (1:3-4), Paul says, "Blessed be the God and Father of our Lord Jesus Christ who hath blessed us with all spiritual blessings . . . as he hath chosen us in him before the foundation of the world . . ."; and in the second chapter he continues, ". . . for we are his workmanship." We are the manifest expression of the Mind of God.

One translation of the Bible (the Dixon Bible) interprets this phrase; "we are his manuscript." Isn't that a wonderful thought! A carpenter expresses his ideas through building with wood and other materials, a gardener through growing plants, a farmer through fields of grain, an inventor expresses his best ideas through the inventions he perfects and gives to the world. God is expressing His thoughts, His ideas, yes, even His hopes, through us, His highest creation, as a writer expresses his thoughts through his writings.

Almost everyone has written a poem at some time. If you have created anything in words, a poem, a news article, an important letter, or a short story, you were expressing something you felt. Whatever it was, you may have wakened in the night, put on the light, and changed a word to give your writing a better meaning. You are God's manuscript, you are God's poem. He created you to express to those who know you some thought of His.

You may have a haunting feeling you have not made of your life all it should be, nor given expression to your deepest yearnings and highest ambitions. Perhaps you have not measured up to the pattern that was in the Mind of God when He created you. Since God remains forever the same, never changing, His pattern for you still exists. By His grace you are privileged to place yourself upon it and be brought more nearly into His likeness.

Glenn Clark, author of twenty books, teacher, and founder of the Camps Farthest Out, used to amuse groups by telling of his family breakfast, where there was much passing of plates for fresh waffles from the baking iron. As usual, there was one waffle which had been baked early, had grown cold, and was pushed aside in favor of a crisp serving. As Glenn looked at this rejected waffle, growing colder and more soggy, he thought of lives as limp as it. Then, while he mused, he saw his wife take the unwanted waffle and place it in the hot iron. After a few minutes it was taken out hot, crisp, and tempting.

"Our lives are like waffles," Glenn would say. "Sometimes we grow cold and limp. We become discouraged and are tempted to give up. We lose confidence in our own abilities as we try to accomplish our work by our own efforts alone. We settle for the mediocre and give up hope for the best. Accepting the good, we lose faith in attaining the excellent. At such times we need to be re-moulded according to God's pattern, even if it requires heat that is necessary to burn out the dross in us."

A song which expresses this feeling is

> Seach me, O God, and know my heart today;
> Try me, O Savior, know my thoughts, I pray;
> See if there be some wicked way in me;
> Cleanse me from every sin, and set me free.

Somewhere, in the march of time, Christians have lost much of the power that was vital to the early Church. Like a branch broken and hanging from the vine which gave it life, the race of struggling humanity languishes for spiritual and physical vitality. We are severed from our Life Source. Deep within, we yearn for abundant life. This is what Jesus came to give. He said, "I am come that they might have life, and that they might have it more abundantly" (Jn. 10:10). When praying to His Father He said, "This is life eternal, that they might know thee the only true God, and Jesus Christ, whom thou hast sent" (Jn. 17:3). As we find our place within the will of God, we are restored to the security for which our hearts yearn.

Was there a time in man's development when the race was motivated by the Great Wisdom, somewhat as lesser forms of life now are? True, God intended man should use the intelligence and free will He gave him, that he should explore and learn the secrets of the world all about him; but it must have been God's intention that man would do this with His help and for the advancement of all people, rather than through selfish struggle that kills and destroys.

Insects, fish, birds, and animals respond to the Great Wisdom that guides them. Insects lay eggs where their young will find food. Fish spawn in places suitable for the protection of their young, the salmon, for instance, going to great effort to return to the waters where life began to reproduce its young. Migrating birds know when to fly South and when to return to their homes in the North. Where is their calendar? What wisdom makes them know the exact time for their departure?

The Capistrano swallows are said to have nested in the ruins of the San Juan Mission in Southern California since early Spanish colonial days, leaving the mission on St. John's Day, October 23rd, and returning on St. Joseph's

Day, March 19th. It is reported that they have been late only once, when they were delayed four hours by a storm at sea.

The behavior of such birds shows that they are guided for their own good by a wisdom beyond their understanding. No wonder Jesus spoke of God's care of the birds, as He said . . . "one of them shall not fall on the ground without your Father" (Matt. 10:29). Then turning to His anxious followers, He reassured them, ". . . ye are of more value than many sparrows" (Matt. 10:31).

Indeed we are of more value than sparrows. Still, through the all-inclusive love of the Creator, the same care which looks after them provides for our needs. The Power which motivates birds and animals is called the Great Wisdom. This same Power, as it develops the body of the human infant and brings it to birth, is called the Great Unconscious. The same Power, as it continues to supervise the functions of our bodies, as our minds allow it to, is called the Life Within.

This Power remains our helper throughout life, as our bodies are kept functioning. Without conscious thought our lungs fill with air, our hearts beat, carrying oxygen to every cell of the body. Even as we sleep, the Life Within is sustaining, renewing, and refreshing every part of our physical being. Stomach and kidneys perform their functions, while every organ has time to repair the effects of strain which has been placed upon it. When there is a wound in the flesh, red corpuscles rush into action to heal, while white corpuscles carry away poison and wall off infection.

All healing must be accomplished within the body. Doctors can dress wounds and apply antiseptics to stop or prevent infection; they can give medication to combat various diseases; but healing must take place in the body, by the body's ability to rebuild and sustain itself.

Humanity is indebted to medical scientists who have given their lives to eliminate many diseases which killed great numbers of people in the past. Diseases such as plague, cholera, smallpox, and various fevers are unknown in our land today, while the great crippler, poliomyelitis, has been halted by more recent research.

Let us co-operate with our doctors, give thanks for their training and skill, and pray for them as they work untiringly to alleviate suffering. Most doctors recognize a Power beyond themselves. They know that when they have done all they can, they must trust the life of their patients to this Power, and hope the Life Within those bodies will bring healing. Doctors recognize the will to live, the value of hope, courage, and optimism in their patients. They welcome prayer when it fosters these, when it uplifts the mind, and in this way aids the healing process.

It is vital to have the service of a reliable doctor when needed. However, each person can be his own best physician as he gives attention to the laws of health and guards against mental attitudes which destroy his well being; as he recognizes the power of God in his life, and allows this Life Within to restore and rebuild daily.

Too much medicine can be as harmful, or more so, as none at all. The amount of pills taken by the American people is appalling. Some take medicine to get to sleep, then take more to wake them up. There is a bottle for every fluctuation of feeling. The witch doctor's potion holds no greater sway over his adherents than does the power of pills over many American people, who are becoming "Pillgrims" on the way of life. People are influenced by what they see and hear. The constant blare of television commercials which advertise drugs is leading many an unsuspecting person to take them when they are not needed.

Remember, young woman-watching-television-while-doing-your-ironing, the advertisements of various medicines, from appetite depressants to headache and sleeping pills, are not made solely for your benefit, but, to a great extent, for business and industrial profits.

Pain is an alarm signal that all is not well in the body. It should lead us to discover what caused it rather than to take a pill to deaden it. Merely stopping the pain may allow the condition which caused it to grow worse, until serious ailments develop and drastic measures, even surgery, may be advised.

Doctor Everts G. Loomis, founder of Friendly Hills Fellowship, a healing center near Hemet, California, said in a lecture, "There are entirely too many surgical operations being performed these days. There is an increasing number of people who seem to think that as soon as they have a new trouble, they can go to a surgeon and have it cut out. As a result of multiple surgery, such persons become greatly weakened, their hormone structure is profoundly affected, and the road to the mental hospital grows increasingly wide."

Perhaps the young woman watching television as she irons feels sick because she is bored. Life has grown monotonous. Marriage is not like the love stories she has read. It seems she has no friends, since she no longer fits into the group of girl friends she used to know. The baby came so soon. She is not mature enough to appreciate having a child; instead he ties her at home. She rubs her hand over her aching head. Poor dear, the foods she eats have been so refined that much of the needed food value has been taken out. The bran which is taken from the flour that makes her bread might help her. A bowl of bran cereal with prunes or other fruit each day should cleanse her system, relieve her headache and enable her to face life more cheerfully.

Perhaps the young woman is lonely. It may be that she and her husband have dropped out of church. They need friends. They might find them among the young couples of a Church School group. While there they could leave the baby in the nursery where he would be well cared for. It would do them both good to dress up and get out with people, to be in circulation together again. Together, in church. Ah, that is a prescription.

Wake up young woman. Find the cause of your tired feeling before you become really sick. To doctor symptoms without making right that which causes them is like rubbing beauty cream over an abscessed tooth.

IV

MEETING THE STRESS OF LIFE

THERE IS NOTHING as powerful as an idea whose time has come," said Victor Hugo. Evidently the time has come for the recognition of the stress of life as a cause of illness.

This truth is dealt with at length by Doctor Hans Selye of Montreal, Canada, in his book, *The Stress of Life.*[1] Like the man who built a better mousetrap, Dr. Selye baited his trap with an idea and the idea is catching on. It makes sense and the world of medical science is beating a path to his door.

Hans Selye was a brilliant youth. He was in medical school in Vienna at the age of eighteen. His father and grandfather were doctors and this was always his field of interest.

Dr. Selye says he never shall forget the first time he watched a doctor demonstrate to students how to examine patients. All those who came for examination were evidently sick. They had fever, sore throats, and ached in

---

[1] McGraw-Hill Book Co., New York.

various parts of the body, but as the doctor examined them, he could find no recognizable disease. So the patients were sent home to wait until they developed a disease which the doctor could treat. No importance seemed to be attached to the syndrome of just being sick. Having an inquisitive mind which was not satisfied to accept what had been handed down to him, Dr. Selye began his search to discover why people are "just sick." After much research and many rebuffs and failures, he finally reached the conclusion that most sickness is caused by stress.

Dr. Selye begins his book by asking, "What is Stress?" and goes on to say,

> The soldier who sustains wounds in battle, the mother who worries about her soldier son, the gambler who watches the races, the horse and the jockey he bet on; they are all under stress. The beggar who suffers hunger and the glutton who overeats, the little shopkeeper with his constant fear of bankruptcy and the rich merchant struggling for yet another million; they are all under stress. The housewife who tries to keep her children out of trouble, the child who scalds himself—and especially the particular cells of the skin over which he poured the boiling coffee—they, too, are under stress.
>
> What is this one mysterious condition that the different kinds of people have in common with animals and even with individual cells, at times when much—much of anything—happens to them? What is the nature of stress? This is the fundamental question of the life of everyone; it touches clearly upon the essence of life and disease. To understand the mechanism of stress gives physicians a new ap-

proach to the treatment of illness, but it can also give us a new philosophy to guide our actions in conformity with natural laws.

Explaining his use of the term, stress, the Doctor says,

For this nocuous agent we needed a fitting name. I again stumbled upon the term "stress" which had long been used in common English, and particularly in engineering to denote forces which act against resistance. For example, the changes induced in a rubber band during traction or in a steel spring during pressure are due to stress.

The Doctor says that some part of the body becomes the *point of resistance* and receives the onslaught of stress. This point of resistance may be the heart in one person, kidneys in another, joints in another person. Any part of the body may become a point of resistance. Whatever irritates is a *stresser*. This might be a burn, it might be bacteria entering the body, or it might be emotion. This stresser reacts on the hypothalamic area of our brain. The hypothalamus is located right in the center of the head, just behind the pituitary gland, which is the key gland of the body.

Dr. Selye explains,

In the tissues more directly affected by stress, there develops a *local adaptation syndrome;* for instance, there is inflammation where microbes enter the body . . . chemical *alarm signals* are sent out by directly stressed tissues from the centers of co-ordination in the *nervous system* and to endocrine glands, especially the *pituitary* and the *adrenals,* which produce *adaptive hormones,* to combat wear and tear in the body . . . The adaptive hormones fall into two groups; the anti-inflammatory hormone and the pro-inflammatory hormone. These should be in balance, but when, if the pro-inflammatory hormone is elaborated in one point of resistance, let us say a knee joint, we have a case of arthritis.

If we could understand what causes illness and have the grace to avoid those things which bring it on, would this not be better than the effort to heal our sickness after they develop?

Experience tells us of the ill effects of stress. Most persons have had experiences in their own lives when the pressure of stress has pushed unrelentingly until they have become sick. Doctors have said that emotional stress often results in stomach ulcers and skin trouble.

Dr. Selye shows clearly how the glands of the body respond to stress. The pituitary gland, which is the master gland of the body, lies close beside the hypothalamus of the brain and is connected to it by a nerve pathway. This responds to thinking and feelings. When one's feelings are wrought up, the pituitary gland receives the impressions sent to it by the brain and transmits these to other glands which carry the feelings of disturbance to other parts of the body.

The liver is a gland, and when the liver is not healthy the disposition shows it. We speak truly when we say, "He makes me sick," "She gives me a pain in the neck," and "I can't stomach" this or that.

The adrenal glands supplied quick energy to primitive man who needed to flee or fight for his life. Today man has the same adrenaline thrown into his blood stream when he is pressed to anger. But if we have nowhere to run and dare not fight, we swell up in anger, get red in the face, sweat, and our throat tightens.

Many persons have sickness in the body which has its roots in emotional stress. They have been pushing against some condition so long that they are exhausted from the continual pressure. When the mind can no longer cope with the stress upon it, the body often will take over and assume the onslaught of stress so as to relieve the mind. This may prevent mental illness. It is helpful co-operation between mind and body. On the other hand, the illness visible in the body sometimes is an expression of mental and emotional frustration.

Mr. Looman was losing the use of his right arm. No physical cause could be found for this problem. The only explanation he could think of was that he wanted so much to punch his boss in the nose that the effort to refrain from doing so seemed to have caused his arm to become lifeless. He left the company and the overseer under whom he had been working, found employment he liked and where he was happy, and his arm got well. He has had no further trouble with his health.

Face trouble. To run from wild animals is to invite a chase. So it is with all trying situations. When these are faced unemotionally, truth usually outweighs error, and good may result.

A boy lies shivering with fright as moonlight casts shadows in his room. A dark form seems to be standing in the doorway looking at him. Imagining it to be a burglar, he covers his head and lies still, his heart pounding. When he peeks again, the menacing thing is still there. For a time he suffers all the torments his imagination can conjure up. At last he musters courage to turn on the light and sees his father's coat hanging on the back of the door.

Dr. Selye put mice in a cage and then allowed a cat to run around it, tormenting them. The mice could not reason that the wire of the cage was protecting them, so they developed ulcers. We have minds with which to reason, but often we make ourselves sick worrying about things that never happen.

A story that evokes laughter is of a woman who sat weeping. Her neighbor asked her what caused her such grief, to which she answered, "I was just thinking that if my Annie got married and had a baby when it got big enough to play in the yard, a tiger might come and tear it to pieces." "Silly. There aren't any tigers in this country," the neighbor scolded. "But what if there was one?" the woman wailed.

There are troubles real and troubles imagined, but of whatever kind they are, things that alarm us should be examined to learn the truth which at times is concealed by our fear.

One experienced psychologist advises his patients to "kiss the monster," or grasp their fears and hug them to their breasts until the mask that conceals their reality is torn away. When fear of anything rises, he says to think of the worst that can happen as a result of the situation, to look at it honestly, and accept it. This destroys its power to hurt us.

In sickness, the worst we can think of is death. Why be terrified by that which must come to all some time? All who have lived and passed on have gone through this gateway. Why go into a panic at the thought of stepping from this life into a fuller and more beautiful existence? We are promised, "Eye hath not seen, nor ear heard, neither have entered into the heart of man, the things which God hath prepared for them that love him" (I Cor. 2:9). How much better it is to think of the joys of heaven which we are promised will exceed our most glorious imaginings. Let your imagination create the heaven that will be the greatest joy for you. Think on happiness and joy, and allow the peace of God to dwell in your heart.

Trouble is inevitable. It comes to all. We must decide how we shall take it, rather than giving way and wringing our hands in despair as we cry, "Why did this have to happen to me?"

One mother cried, "Where was God when my son was killed in battle?" God was the same as He was when His own Son died on the cross. Since God did not spare Himself, nor His Son, can we expect that He shall spare us all suffering? Wars are not of God's making, but are devised by men. God must be doing the best He can within the situations that are of man's making. Dr. E. Stanley Jones, missionary of world renown, was asked why God allowed His children to suffer, why good people were not exempt. Dr. Jones answered that if God spared his children from suffering, they would not be His children but His spoiled brats.

By meeting difficulties and overcoming them, we grow in character. If we accept the hurts of life and through them become more understanding and helpful toward others, then suffering becomes for us a blessing. Troubles are the weights we lift to strengthen our spiritual muscles. Paul likened the race of life to the Olympic Games of his day. In life, however, everyone is engaged in the race. Life is a game to be played, a race to be run. If we are to become strong we must accept the hurdles. Gymnasiums are not equipped with rocking chairs.

If, at times, we feel like saying with James Russell Lowell, "Truth forever on the scaffold, wrong forever on the throne," we must go on and realize, "but the scaffold sways the future and beyond the dim unknown, standeth God within the shadows, keeping watch above His own."

The first day of school a mother accompanies her son to the school house. The second day she takes him across the street and cautions him to look in all directions to make sure no cars are approaching before he starts across the road way. The third morning the mother goes down the front walk with her son, and tells him he is a big boy and must cross the road by himself. She assures him he can do this if he will give strict attention to all she has taught him. Now she leaves him to decide when to start across the street.

After his mother leaves, the boy stands alone watching the automobiles whiz by. He feels alone, inadequate, and thinks for a moment of running into the house to his mother and telling her he cannot do this alone. But pride bolsters his courage. He knows his mother trusts him, and he does not want to fail her. The boy is growing up.

But the mother does not go into the house and begin her morning work when she leaves her son to make his own decision. Ah, no. Far from it. The mother steps behind an arborvitae bush, where she is hidden from the child yet where she can watch his every move. She also watches the street, up and down, to see if cars are approaching. Her heart is in her mouth. She clenches her fists and bites her lips as her mother instinct cries out to go to him, but her good sense tells her to be still and allow the child to start on the road to becoming a man.

Perhaps God who "standeth in the shadows keeping watch above His own" may feel this same concern for us, but having given us free will, He allows us to make our own mistakes and to learn through them, that in doing so we may advance on the road to maturity.

V

FAITH IN JESUS BRINGS HEALING

JESUS HEALED when He lived in the flesh, and He heals today. So many healings have been verified that the question is not, are such healings possible? but, how are they accomplished? How can we find an answer to this question in any better way than by studying the account of Jesus' words and acts of healing as recorded in the Gospels? Wouldn't it have been wonderful to have walked with Jesus and listened to Him speak, to have been present when He healed the lepers, the lame, the blind, and crippled, and to have seen them spring up and go their way rejoicing? You can make these characters live. As the story comes alive to your mind and heart, Jesus will grow more real to you.

Select a story of one of Jesus' healings. Read it from every translation of the Gospels you have. Decide which you like best, then read it again and again, thoughtfully and prayerfully, until you seem to be a part of it. Listen to Jesus' words with all your mind and heart. Respond to His questions and commands as if His eyes were looking intently into yours.

Now relax. Let this story unfold in your mind as on a motion picture screen. Create the setting. See the people involved, and especially see Jesus as He moves and speaks. Jesus usually spoke in parables. As people listened to His stories, they heard more than His words for they identified themselves with the characters He portrayed. Men saw themselves tilling fields, sowing grain, buying and selling land, pulling oxen out of ditches, and tending sheep. Women saw themselves kneading bread, sweeping floors, hunting for lost treasures, and going to weddings. All felt concern for a lost sheep, and their hearts beat faster as He told of a lost boy.

In Psalm 34, verse 3 reads: "O magnify the Lord with me, and let us exalt his name together." When a picture is magnified, it is made large so that every detail can be clearly seen. Let us magnify, that is, enlarge and fill in details of the story we select for a mental motion picture.

In Mark (1:29-31) we find three short verses that tell us, "When they were come out of the synagogue, they entered into the house of Simon and Andrew with James and John. But Simon's wife's mother lay sick of a fever, and anon they tell him of her. And he came and took her by the hand, and lifted her up; and immediately the fever left her, and she ministered unto them."

Here in sixty words is a thrilling story. When you magnify it, fill in details, and give it color, you can make it come to life. Try it and see. Go back to the meeting of Jesus and Peter. Remember it was Peter's brother, Andrew, who first met Jesus and brought these two together. Read Matthew 4:18, which tells of Jesus meeting these brothers by the sea, as does Mark in the first chapter, beginning at the sixteenth verse.

One day a man named Andrew met Jesus. He was so

captivated by Jesus that he took Him to meet his brother
Simon Peter. Visualize Peter, a rugged fisherman, by his
fishing boat on the sea shore. What did this rough man,
accustomed to nets and fish, think of Jesus? As he looked
into this man's eyes he must have seen the best in himself—
all he had dreamed of and hoped to become. This man who
had spent his life catching fish heard the command, "Follow me, and I will make you a fisher of men." Then Peter
left his nets and followed Jesus.

No doubt Peter and Andrew invited Jesus to their home,
and also James and John. Peter's mother-in-law was feeling
miserable with a fever. She was so ill she was not able to
be the gracious hostess for Peter's guests. Here was a
mother-in-law that had the love and respect of her family.
Peter would have been proud to have introduced her to his
friends. He did not try to conceal her condition. The four
men could have gone into the living room with Jesus and
waited until supper was ready, disregarding the sick mother,
but rather, "they tell him of her." Jesus came, took her by
the hand, and lifted her up; immediately the fever left her.

How much these few words tell. Here is compassion and
concern. Here is a guest who is also a physician. As the
elderly mother was able to go about her accustomed duty
of serving the evening meal, the happiness in her heart must
have been shared by all who sat at the table. That night the
supper must have expressed the proverb, "Better is a dinner
of herbs where love is, than a stalled ox and hatred there-
with" (Prov. 15:17).

(In every home He visited, Jesus seemed to put those
about Him at ease. Mary, who wanted only to sit at His
feet and listen to His words, realized that to be with Him
was a greater feast than carefully served foods.)

Notice in the story of the healing of Simon's wife's mother

that Jesus "took her by the hand." Jesus knew the value of the friendly touch. He put out His hands to lepers, never drawing away in fear of physical contact with them. He did not seem afraid of catching what they had, for that which He had was so much greater that it went out from Him in cleansing and healing power.

Think of this story. Get the feel of it. Visualize the various characters. Sense the relief and joy of the mother's healing, and think of the tender compassion of Jesus.

As you bring to life the characters in this Bible story you are putting into action one of the mental faculties most unused by many adults—the imagination. Artists, writers, inventors, and builders make use of this power to imagine, but most of us seem to think this is a form of childish day-dreaming. Before a book is written, it takes form in the mind of the author. Before a building rises or a bridge spans a stream, they are first conceived in the mind of him who plans them. Before a work of faith is realized, it is grasped as a possibility.

Jesus asked, "Do you believe I can do this?" Let us para-phrase this question as, Can you conceive in your imagina-tion that which you desire as a finished work of God? Do you hold in your mind the belief that God is able, through Christ, to heal you, and can you create a picture of yourself healed? If so, you are a candidate for healing. If not, perhaps your imagination is atrophied. Children go adven-turing on wings of imagination. Become like a little child, as Jesus advised, and soar on wings of thought.

Turn now to the story of the woman who touched the hem of Jesus' robe and see how well you can become

identified with her. After studying the story told in the
ninth chapter of Matthew, relax and create on the screen
of your mind the setting for the action. See the blue sky
with white clouds, the ash-gray earth, sparse vegetation,
bushes and clumps of grass. Over a hill winds a narrow
road made by cart wheels and donkey's feet. On this road
a crowd of people moves. The curious spectators surge
about a dozen men who seem to be trying to protect the
man in the center of the group from the throng about Him.
Oh look! It is the Master, Jesus of Nazareth, who travels
today. He has been called to the home of the nobleman,
Jairus, to minister to his little daughter and is on his way
there. See the Master in the midst of the crowd, his face
serene and lifted in the warm sunshine. He smiles and
speaks to those who address Him as the company moves on.

But wait. The Master stops. He looks about him, his
expression alert, questioning. One account of the story
reads: "And Jesus, immediately knowing in himself that
virtue had gone out of him, turned him about in the press,
and said, Who touched my clothes?" (Mk. 5:30)

Realizing how the people were pushing on every side,
the disciples questioned why Jesus would ask who touched
Him. They would have gone on, but Jesus moved not a
step. As he waited expectantly, the crowd parted and a
poor, emaciated woman crept up to Jesus and fell at his
feet. Her hands folded in supplication, her tearful face
lifted toward this one whom she has sought, she pours
out the story of her affliction. For twelve years she had
suffered from a hemorrhage. All her money had been spent
with doctors but to no avail. In her extremity, she believed
that if she might get to the prophet Jesus and could only
touch the hem of His garment, she would be healed. She

had made her way to Him. She had touched his cloak. Now she waited humbly, ready to receive whatever the Teacher might give her.

This was a tense moment. Perhaps some in the crowd held their breath. What would the Master say after being rudely stopped when He was on His way to answer the call of a nobleman? This was an important mission. Would He resent the intrusion and be scornful toward the intruder? What would He say to her? Would He call her "beggar"? At best He might address her as "woman."

But wait! See the compassion on His face. How could a man's face reflect such love; especially when he had been interrupted—and by a bedraggled creature with scarcely enough strength to drag herself before Him. Beggars were common in that country and usually were scorned.

The crowd grew quiet, watching. The disciples were tense, waiting for Jesus' response. Then Jesus spoke one magic word. As he was to use the name, "Mary," in the garden on Easter morning, He now uttered one word which changed the entire drama. With the tenderness of a fond parent speaking to a beloved child, He said, "Daughter."

Daughter! Surely the woman was breathless, overcome by love. By thus naming her, Jesus lifted her to a place equal to Himself. He called her daughter! She was recognized as a descendant of Abraham, the ancient tribal father whose lineage was the pride of the Hebrew people. But He had also lifted her to a place beside Himself as a child of God whom he called Father. No wonder her affliction was instantly cured. With such love and acceptance she was made well and her whole life must have been transformed.

Notice that Jesus did not say His grace had healed her, even though He was conscious that power had gone from

Him. Instead He looked at the woman and said, "Thy faith hath made thee whole."

What a strange thing to say when Jesus knew that power from God had gone from Him and had entered into this woman and resulted in her healing. Why did He say it was her faith that had made her whole? While it is God's will to heal, there must also be a seeking, a rising up to receive this healing, on the part of man. Here is the key to divine healing.

The powerful vibration which leaves the sun is transformed and becomes light only when it reaches the atmosphere of earth and infuses a substance which the earth sends out to meet it. When these two merge, light is manifest. In the same manner, electricity comes down from the clouds and merges with the electricity which goes up from the ground resulting in a flash of lightning. So the boundless power of God must find faith in man before any work of divine healing can be accomplished. This is a divine-human reciprocity, a give and take that results in healing.

This truth, this unbroken law holds. When anyone is healed by prayer, someone, somewhere has had faith in God and someone, or many have prayed. Such prayer often is made by persons other than the patient who is healed, but usually the one who seeks healing exercises his faith in order to give power to the inflow of God's healing grace.

Again and again Jesus verified this truth. He asked those who came to Him seeking healing, "Do you believe I can do this?" He confirmed it, as He said to those who did believe, "Go in peace, your faith has made you whole," and "As you believe, so be it unto you."

How graciously Jesus entered into the troubled lives of people of His day. How competent He was, how sure of the power of God which flowed through Him as He stretched forth His hand to heal. That divine power is the same today as we turn to Him in our need. God is the same, yesterday, today, and forever. Jesus Christ is alive, a Presence in the world; invisible, yes, but very real, as real as goodness and love are real. We call to Him in our need and He hears our call.

VI

YOUR SINS ARE FORGIVEN

ANOTHER HEALING that points up the faith of the person who was sick, and especially of the friends who had his interest at heart, is that of the man so crippled of palsy that he was not able to get to Jesus by himself. This man's friends had such faith that they carried him, using a quilt for a stretcher, to the house where Jesus was speaking. When they found there a crowd so great that they could not get to the door, they climbed onto the roof, loosened a portion of it, and let their helpless friend down through the opening until he rested at Jesus' feet.

Looking at the man before Him, then up at his friends who had carried him there, Jesus took in the entire situation. But He saw deeper than the sick man's need of healing. As he "knew what was in man," Jesus realized this man's greatest need was for forgiveness of sins.

As kindly as he had spoken to the woman who touched his cloak and using a term as complimentary as that He used when speaking to her, Jesus said, "Son, thy sins be forgiven thee" (Mk. 2:5).

Knowing the thoughts in the minds of many who stood looking on, He said to them, ". . . is it easier to say to the sick of the palsy, Thy sins be forgiven thee; or to say, Arise, and take up thy bed, and walk? But that ye may know that the Son of man hath power on earth to forgive sins, (he saith to the sick of the palsy,) . . . Arise, and take up thy bed, and go thy way into thine house" (Mk. 2:9-11). Imagine the doubters' consternation as they saw the crippled man stand up, pick up his quilt, and, straight of back and limbs, walk away.

That man would not have been healed if it had not been for those who cared enough to bring him directly to Jesus. How often friends carry the needs of an ailing one, lifting him in faith and persisting in prayer until he is healed. How important friends are! When one is so ill that his mind cannot hold steady in prayer, those who love him can uphold him while exercising faith for him. It is important that the one convalescing does not become discouraged.

Many persons have received a true healing through prayer but have returned to their homes where they are surrounded by unbelieving neighbors, who shake their heads and voice their doubts that a lasting healing has taken place. How valuable are friends who believe God, and who will strengthen the faith of the one whose healing is in progress. Most healings are progressive, as was true of the person Jesus touched: "From that same hour he began to mend." When one is healed through prayer, someone or many have prayed and believed. Truly "the effectual fervent prayer of a righteous man availeth much."

Another important observation to make in the story of the man carried to Jesus by his friends is Jesus' discernment of the man's greatest need, which was that his sins be forgiven. Here Jesus touched the deepest need of all mankind. Many times we seek healing for our bodies when the need of our lives is for forgiveness of sins.

The sin that most often blocks healing is the sin of resentment and unforgiveness. Jesus was positive when He spoke of the necessity of forgiving others their trespasses against us. Is this not the very center of the prayer He taught His disciples? In this He taught them to pray: "Forgive us our debts, as we forgive our debtors" (Matt. 6:12). When Peter asked Jesus, "Lord, how oft shall my brother sin against me, and I forgive him? till seven times?" Jesus replied, "I say not unto thee, Until seven times: but Until seventy times seven" (Matt. 18:21-22).

Resentment and hate held against others eat into our own hearts and keep us from fellowship with God. It is impossible to worship God with a clean heart when harboring hate and resentment, and it is as difficult to receive healing from God when there is resentment in our lives. Resentment is the sin that must be forgiven before we can "rise and walk."

Notice that Jesus told the paralyzed man who lay before Him to get up. The man may have reasoned that he couldn't get up. It may have been years since he had stood on his feet. He may have looked at his withered limbs and have told himself it was impossible to get up. But Jesus said, "Arise," and the man arose. Jesus said, "Take up your bed." The man knowing he had not lifted anything for months may have opened his mouth in astonishment, but he picked up his pallet. Jesus said, "Walk," and the man walked.

Jesus says to every drooping spirit, "Arise." This is a first necessity in healing. We must bestir ourselves out of our lethargy and expect a miracle. Jesus calls every one who wants to be well to use every bit of faith he has and to exert every ounce of energy within him. He must "Arise."

He may need first of all to stand up on the inside, to be filled with the purpose and the will to arise from sickness and to stand, by the Grace of God, in health. This may mean to exercise an attitude of health. Think health, picture health, accept healing, and stand up in the assurance of it. When Jesus spoke, men obeyed. He speaks today. He tells us, "Do what you can, rise from your lethargy, use your body, and expect it to become well, do everything you know to increase life within you."

I was called to pray for a woman who was bedfast. When I entered her room it was stifling hot, the temperature around ninety degrees. Every window was closed. All the fresh air that got into the room crept in when the door was opened. The woman lay among pillows, smelling of liniment and moaning. She had given up trying to be well. Poor dear, she wanted sympathy. I was sorry for her, sorry she had not mustered the courage to act when wisdom said, "Get out of bed and walk." It was necessary to minister to this woman's mind before trying to heal her body. Carefully, kindly, I talked with her of the life of God within her and of her ability to respond to this healing life. There had to be awakened in her the will to live, which came as she saw some purpose in life and a usefulness for herself. Like many others, she had turned her mind within and withdrawn from active participation with others. Sinking down and lying limp, this woman has refused to "walk."

If people would only walk, they might prevent many illnesses. Automobiles have stolen the function of our legs. We ride three blocks, even one, rather than walk. We were made for walking. Those who walk in the fresh air every day fill their lungs with oxygen, which increases circulation and stimulates the brain. Walking out of one's house and closing the door on its demands refreshes the spirit. They who walk outrun many petty irritations.

Jesus uttered a prescription for health when He said to arise, take up whatever you are leaning on and walk. Of course He gave the man to whom He spoke strength to do what He asked of him. He will give us strength, too, and forgive us for our very lethargy when we trust Him, turn about, and exert our will power and common sense. We must make a constant, consistent effort to renew our health by the use of resources at hand. "Though your sins be as scarlet, they shall be as white as snow." When we turn to Him and work with Him our whole beings respond magnificently. Fresh air, sunshine, clear water, natural foods with preference for fruits and vegetables rather than sugar and starches, proper elimination, sufficient rest, and an attitude of hopeful expectancy all work together toward abundant health, and will produce many a cure.

VII

THE POWER OF THE SPOKEN WORD

THE POWER of the spoken word is shown in the story of the centurion, a captain in the Roman Army, who came to Jesus in behalf of his servant whom, he said, "lieth at home sick of the palsy, grievously tormented."

This centurion probably was stationed in Capernaum, a city where Jesus spent much time and where many of His mighty works were done. The centurion must have been well known here for he had built the Jews a synagogue (*cf.* Lk. 7:5). Yet he did not mention this, but expressed humility as the two men stood together. After hearing of the need of the servant who suffered at home and seeing the concern of his master, Jesus said, "I will come and heal him." To this the Army officer replied, "Lord, I am not worthy that thou shouldest come under my roof: but speak the word only, and my servant shall be healed. For I am a man under authority, having soldiers under me: and I say to this man, Go, and he goeth; and to another, Come, and

he cometh; and to my servant, Do this and he doeth it"
(Matt. 8:5-9).

Here was a man who had authority in the Roman Army
and who recognized Jesus as having authority in another
realm. When this man gave an order, soldiers under him
promptly obeyed without questioning. When he gave a
command his servants carried out that command. A man
whose words are obeyed knows the power of the spoken
word. Now this man of Rome stood beside the man of
Galilee, recognizing in Him the same authority, and saying,
"Speak the word only, and my servant shall be healed."

Did this man see what the multitudes failed to see in
Jesus? Did he know that unseen forces were available to
do His bidding, that legions of angels were at His command? When the crowd, guided by Judas, came with
swords and staves to take Jesus in Gethsemane, He told
them He could call twelve legions of angels to His aid
(Matt. 26:53). All the hosts of Heaven were at attention
as the Son of God carried out His mission on earth. As a
man, he used only the resources which are available to
men, never breaking into the realm of the divine to use
such power solely for His own good or to demonstrate His
glory. Such restraint Jesus must have used, knowing "All
power is given unto me in heaven and in earth," as He
said (Matt. 28:18). When alone in the wilderness after fast-
ing forty days, there where no mortal man ever would have
known He did it, He refused to use heavenly power to turn
stones into bread for himself. Yet to feed hungry people
who might faint by the roadside, He multiplied a handful
of bread and fish to feed thousands.

The secret of the power that, later, lay pulsing all around
Him as He suffered humiliation at the hands of crude,

ignorant, and wicked humans, now seemed to be glimpsed by a man not of His race, nor of His religion. As Jesus looked into the face of this soldier He must have seen the universality of His Father's kingdom and to have known, even as we are learning today, that all wisdom is not vested in any one race, color, or creed, but that all men are one in God.

When Jesus heard the words of the Centurion He marveled and said to them that stood by, "Verily I say unto you, I have not found so great faith, no, not in Israel." Jesus went on to say that many should come from the east and the west and sit down with Abraham, Isaac, and Jacob in the Kingdom of Heaven, but the children of the kingdom should be cast out. The Kingdom of Heaven is for those who obey the authority of the King rather than for those born of some race or family. The authority of this Kingdom is the Word of the King.

Is this Word a small thing? No, it is an earth shaking thing. It was by the Word of God the heavens and all that is in them were formed: "God said, Let there be light: and there was light" (Gen. 1:3). The Word of God became man and dwelt among us. This Word was Christ Jesus. John states this in the first chapter of his Gospel: "In the beginning was the Word, and the Word was with God, and the Word was God. The same was in the beginning with God. All things were made by him; and without him was not anything made that was made. In him was life; and the life was the light of men." This incarnation of God's Word now stood beside a Roman soldier who said, ". . . speak the word only and my servant shall be healed."

Jesus used God's word, quoting the Scriptures, to defeat Satan when He was tempted in the wilderness. He said,

"Man shall not live by bread alone, but by every word that proceedeth out of the mouth of God" (Matt. 4:4). The Word is healing, the Word is sustenance, the Word is life.

People who memorize passages of Scripture have a weapon with which to meet temptations. Like the Psalmist they can say, "Thy word have I hid in mine heart, that I might not sin against thee"; and "Thy word is a lamp unto my feet, and a light unto my path" (Ps. 119:11, 105).

The Centurion who came to Jesus may not have known the extent of the influence of the spoken word, but Jesus knew. His commendation of the man proves this. We are learning something of the power of words which are spoken with feeling. Words can be helpful or harmful. They can build up or destroy.

Words of gossip can damage character. Repeated words of hear say may start an avalanche that ends in destruction. Words spoken in anger can sear a sensitive soul. Words of criticism may blight like fire. Such words can hurt the one criticized, but they return like a boomerang to pierce the heart of him who spoke them. Harsh words spoken in anger under provocation can cause children to withdraw from free communication with those who have scolded them. Words of condemnation blast hopes. Words of hate raise barriers which may never be let down.

Words also inspire. Comforting words gladden the heart. Words of confidence inspire renewed efforts. Words of goodwill create harmony. Words of tolerant understanding make for peace. Words of encouragement can change the life of one in despair. Words of concern lift the lonely. Words of confidence strengthen the weak. Words of happiness cheer the sad. Words of love strengthen family relationships. Words of sympathy comfort those who mourn.

Words of patience inspire those about to give up. Words of hope lift tired eyes toward a better tomorrow. And words of Christian love point to Him whose words are life. Simple, sincere words of faith raised to God in love and confidence can bring His healing.

Truly, "a word fitly spoken is like apples of gold in pictures of silver" (Prov. 25:11).

VIII

THE GREAT PSYCHIATRIST

Jesus IS CALLED the Great Physician, and so He is, but He is also the Great Psychiatrist. He understood people, and it is written that He often knew what was in their minds before they voiced their thoughts. The Scripture indicates He knew what the onlookers were thinking after He said to the man let down through the roof, "Thy sins are forgiven."

To heal a physical sickness without healing that which is causing it is only a temporary cure, for the illness usually returns when its cause remains. Deep feelings rooted in the emotions often are the cause of sickness. Knowing this, Jesus ministered to the minds and spirits of those He healed making them "every whit whole." "Whit" means the smallest particle and "whole" means complete. So when Jesus healed He must have left His patients completely well.

Dislike, resentment, and hatred are the roots of much illness, and Jesus tried to eliminate these from persons around Him. He understood the Jews' attitude toward people whose country bordered Palestine. Their feeling was so strong toward the Samaritans that they would travel around that country rather than pass through it. The enmity between Ishmael and Isaac, the two sons of Abraham, had been kept alive for centuries and often erupted in wars, as each race fought for the land they felt was rightfully theirs as descendants of their father.

When Jesus was asked, "Who is my neighbor?" He told a story of a man, a Jew, on his way to Jericho who was beaten, robbed and left bleeding by the roadside. A priest and a Levite—both Jews—passed by without helping him. It was none other than a Samaritan who stopped, bound up the man's wounds, took him to an inn, paid for his keep, and promised to pay for any additional expenses. Then Jesus asked, "Which of these was neighbor to the man who fell among thieves?" This story was more powerful than any argument would have been.

Jesus traveled many places with His disciples. They might have passed around the country from which Jesus' Good Samaritan came, but the Gospel explains that Jesus "must needs go through Samaria" (Jn. 4:4). Jesus had a purpose there.

Stopping at a certain well, Jesus sent His men to buy food while He sat on the well curb and waited until one of the villagers came to draw water. Jesus' purpose here was to tell the Good News of God's love to the people of the nearby village, and this Samaritan woman was the key person who could bring them to hear Him.

(Bishop K. C. Pillai, who was born in India, in his book, *Light Through an Eastern Window,* clarifies many errors which were made by scribes of the West when the Bible was translated into English because they did not understand Oriental customs which prevailed when the original manuscripts were written. The Bishop says this woman of Samaria has been defamed by these translators.[1] The pas-

---

[1] *Light Through An Eastern Window,* Bishop K. C. Pillai, Robert Speller and Sons, New York, N.Y., p. 92.

sage (see Jn. 4:18) should read, "the man who is now courting you," rather than "the man whom thou now hast is not thy husband." This was not an immoral woman, but a strong person, respected in her city so much so that she could call the entire population to see and hear one whom she recommended.)

This woman evidenced a keen mind. She asked intelligent questions, and Jesus talked to her about deep things: about living water; about true worship—worship which is in spirit and in truth. It was to her He spoke the great truth: "God is a Spirit." She listened, she accepted, and she called her friends to hear.

Returning, the disciples were amazed that Jesus would talk to a Samaritan woman. But Jesus valued persons for their own worth. His actions disregarded customs of His time.

The story told in Matthew 15:22-28 reveals Jesus as the Great Psychiatrist. In this drama, we find Him caught in a tug-of-war between a Syrophoenician woman and the Jewish men who were with Him. Some might think Jesus was out of character here, that He was harsh, and that this story would not strengthen the faith of persons desiring to be healed. I disagree. This story contains deep psychological truth which uncovers much within ourselves that we may be reluctant to admit, but which we would do well to face honestly.

This woman was a descendant of the old Phoenicians of Syria, and, living near Palestine as the Samaritans did, she undoubtedly felt as much enmity toward them as they felt toward all people whose land bordered theirs. No doubt her pride was deeply hurt because the Jews called her people dogs. But, in hope of finding help for her child, she went to this Jewish prophet whom she had heard healed people, hoping that, in spite of her nationality, He might heal her daughter.

While the Greek woman followed Jesus and continued to call for help, His disciples did not conceal their attitude toward her. The Great Psychiatrist, well aware of what was in the minds of those around him, walked calmly on, saying not a word. A form of therapy used by psychiatrists is to allow patients to talk, and talk, until they have worked through surface irritations and finally penetrated to the cause of their emotional disturbance. In this way the doctor probes the deep mind of his patient, getting everything that disturbs him to the surface, until he finally is able to uncover the cause of the patient's illness and help him to overcome it. This was what Jesus was doing. To help the Greek woman recognize her resentment He touched a sore spot by saying, "I am not sent but unto the lost sheep of the House of Israel."

The Jewish disciples voiced their resentment. "Send her away; for she crieth after us," they demanded in protest against her. Back and forth the tug-of-war went on with the Psychiatrist in the middle. When the woman seemed calm, Jesus must have known that deep resentment still was harbored in her heart, and once again He put His prodding finger on this sore spot as He said, "It is not meet to take the children's bread, and to cast it to dogs."

Oh, what a rebuke. How could Jesus, who was so kind and compassionate to the sick, say such a thing? How can a surgeon cut into human flesh? He can because at times such measures are necessary to save life. So Jesus' words cut into the age-old enmity this woman had inherited from her ancestors. And it was effective.

Be it said to this woman's praise that she did not turn

away and whine in self pity. She must have felt the rebuff like a whip lash, but she did not allow her personal feelings to deter her. She was motivated by a purpose which was more important than personal feelings. "Truth, Lord: yet the dogs eat of the crumbs which fall from their masters' table," the woman answered.

This woman had followed Jesus asking Him to heal her daughter. The Great Psychiatrist must have known that the mother needed to be healed of emotional blocks before healing could reach her daughter. He kept drawing her out, letting her talk, until she finally realized her own need and changed her request to "Lord, help *me.*"

This could be the key to many healings if we who pray were perceptive enough and honest enough to grasp it. We ask God to change other people as we try to pick splinters out of their eyes, while the beams in our own blind us to our faults and lead us to deny responsibility for our mistakes. The weak try to evade responsibility by placing the blame for every fault and failure on others. We may call this human nature, but it is the weakness of human nature to evade responsibility for our actions, like Adam who said, "The woman thou gavest to be with me, she gave me of the tree," or like Eve, who whined, "The serpent beguiled me, and I did eat" (Gen. 3:12, 13). The weakness of human nature has not changed since the Garden of Eden. Blame still is placed on women, on the Devil, even on God.

A mark of maturity is the ability to stand up and say, "I am to blame." Psychiatrists say the most mature words ever spoken were the words of Jesus from His cross, "Father, forgive them; for they know not what they do." In His anguish He not only forgave His persecutors but pleaded their lack of understanding as the cause of their actions.

This was the response of a mature man toward His enemies; indeed, that of the most highly developed man the world has ever known.

No doubt the Syrophoenician woman was healed as well as her daughter, for God does not do things halfway. Mothers are closely allied with their children. Emotional stress in the family is easily picked up by young children. When a child is sick, it is well to look to the conditions in the home. Adults, old and tough, may be able to squabble and wrangle and yet survive, but the dross of bitterness is drained off into the children, who are still tender and sensitive, and they give way under the stress.

Children copy their parents, so of course the parents greatly influence their children's lives. Children will appreciate the true values of life if they see their parents enjoying them. When church attendance is a part of the family life, accepted as important as day school and appreciated and enjoyed by parents, church becomes a natural part of the child's life. When parents are good neighbors, kind and generous, giving attention, interest, and funds to help those about them, their children usually consider these things to be a part of good living.

Psychiatrists point out some emotions which all people face and must overcome if they are to live victoriously. The first of these is fear. It has been said that the infant is born with two basic fears: the fear of falling and the fear of loud noises. Fears increase as the child runs into things that hurt him, and as he learns the fears of those around him. Adults may have fears about the worthwhileness of life itself, about money, illness, fears that they may lose their jobs, that disaster may strike, fear of what people may say about them, fear that the bottom may fall out of our security.

Sometimes the crust on which we stand does give way, but the bottom never falls out for a Christian. When the flimsy crust caves in, he who has Christ finds himself standing on the Rock of Ages.

For many, as mentioned before, the greatest of all fears is the fear of death. It lurks in the dark corners of every heart until Christ dispels it. It is the fear of the unknown and the certainty of approaching it. But the Christian need not fear death. Christ conquered this enemy and said to us, "Because I live, ye shall live also" (Jn. 14:19).

Another destructive force is hate. This can undermine happiness. Hate usually rises in any individual when his supremacy is threatened. It rises to protect the Ego, so hate is self-centeredness. The bigger the "I," the more readily he hates. A child may be angry and strike out at any person who provokes him, but a mature person will take no offense if, for instance a child acts ugly, for he reasons the child acts so because he is immature. So while he overlooks the child's bad behavior, he turns him from anger by his own happy attitude. A spiritually and mentally mature person will do the same thing when immature adults act toward him in a childish way.

Jesus spoke often of the need for forgiveness. A man came to me once asking that I pray for an illness. While talking with me, he mentioned he had not spoken to his brother for thirteen years. He admitted that this enmity caused their mother much distress, but showed no inclination toward reconciliation. I could only think of Jesus telling Peter to forgive seventy times seven. We may excuse our hates and call them dislikes, resentments, and incompatabilities, but we seldom deceive ourselves, and we never deceive God.

A feeling of inferiority causes many people distress. Be

assured that most persons suffer from this sensitivity. Many who strut and swagger do so to cover up a weakness they do not want others to see. A feeling of inferiority is not harmful. It has a good basis. Man needs to recognize his inferiority before God. When he honestly does this and relinquishes his weakness to Him, God empowers him with a greater strength. Sensitive persons are best able to express goodness and love. They do not act so haughty and arrogant that others feel uncomfortable around them, but, knowing their own weaknesses, they modestly minimize their own abilities while emphasizing those of others. No wonder they have many friends. Nothing makes people more happy than to be considered important and to be complimented. Persons with a natural sensitivity often become the center of adoring friends. They give, rather than demand attention.

Surely this is the heart of happiness—to live in the midst of genial friends, one with them, giving, receiving, sharing, loving, and laughing; being a part of the best in one's community and church; and seeing the good in others to reflect this good. Giving kindly to others one's own best is magnified. Withdrawal from society is a symptom of illness. Those who give up and retreat into isolation, or go to bed, pull themselves away from the stream of life. Alone they shrivel, dry up, and die.

The Christian way of life is the way of consideration for others and sharing with others. Jesus indicated that love of God is expressed through love of one's fellowmen: "Inasmuch as ye have done it unto one of the least of these my brethren, ye have done it unto me." Modern psychiatrists agree with the Great Psychiatrist in this. Indeed, as they study Jesus, He comes to be the greatest among them.

Carl Jung, the great Swiss pioneer of the age of psychology, said he had not had a patient over thirty-five years of age whose problem was not basically a religious one. Fritz Kunkel, the German physician-scientist, who was noted for his attempts to unify the findings of Freud and Jung, had given little thought to religion, but one day he picked up the New Testament to see what this man Jesus had to say. Dr. Kunkel not only found Jesus the psychologist, but he found Jesus the Christ. He became an ardent Christian. He lectured widely and wrote many books about psychology in the light of Christian teachings.

In his book *In Search of Maturity* he said, "Jesus of Nazareth was the greatest psychologist of all time . . . All non-religious depth psychology, as well as shallow psychologism, fail to understand man's futile and dangerous position. It does not see that there is a deeper kind of anxiety, not representing the negative aspect of human relationship but the negative relationship to God . . . A new and real relationship to God is the only way out . . . But we have only one book that gives us a full description of the human situation and of the way leading through all trouble and frustration, and finally into the utmost light. It is the great textbook of depth-psychology, the New Testament. Without this religious knowledge we cannot cure the most serious cases of anxiety and compulsive neuroses. We cannot help the dying person to face death, and we cannot hope to master the collective dark powers that threaten human culture today." [2]

---

[2] *In Search of Maturity,* Fritz Kunkel, Charles Scribner's Sons, New York, pp. 12, 27, 28.

IX

ASK, SEEK, KNOCK, AND BELIEVE

I‍F A TRUTH is to be effective it must be established in our subconscious minds, for here is the place of the feelings and emotions which largely prompt our actions. As was pointed out in the illustration of the Man on the Ground Floor and the Partner in the Basement, we see the value of harmony between the conscious and the subconscious mind.

The Partner in the Basement is much like a child and is influenced by repetition. Children like to hear stories told over and over again. When you tell a well-known story to a small child, he is likely to say, "Tell it again." In the same way the Partner who is our Deep Mind must be told again and again all ideas and truths which we wish to instill in our thinking.

Although little was known of the subconscious mind in past ages, the ancients learned the value of repetition. Liturgies were used in worship, as articles of faith were voiced by the congregation. Although the worshippers may not have realized it, they were establishing these beliefs in their subconscious minds as they spoke them with their conscious consent.

People of many religious faiths practice repetition in their worship. The church services of Roman Catholics and Episcopalians, especially, are full of it. Laymen as well as clergy recite prayers and psalms in many Protestant Churches. Students of Christian Science read the same verses from their Bible and text book every day of the week, then go to church on Sunday and listen to two persons read the same verses again. If any of us work seriously to establish in our minds the promises of God as given us in the Bible, we surely will receive His reward.

Rose Allen was a woman of strong character who used psychology effectively. Arthritis was crippling her until she was afraid she might not be able to continue her work. She had been told that there was no cure for arthritis so she knew if she was to regain her health she must not expect to receive it from drugs.

A prayer for healing had brought no immediate relief, so with perseverance Rose set about to do as Paul advised: ". . . work out your own salvation with fear and trembling" (Phil. 2:12). She admitted the fear and often felt the trembling, so she laughingly says, "I knew I was on the right track for I qualified."

She began to search the New Testament, and discovered that God's promises hinge on provisions or actions we ourselves must take. The key seemed to be: "If ye abide in me, and my words abide in you, ye shall ask what ye will, and it shall be done unto you" (Jn. 15:7). The provision here was that she first must abide, live, make her home in God, and secondly that Jesus' words must live, even come to life in her as she put them into practice.

As she began this program to regain her health, she made a covenant with God that she would do her best to live up to the standards set forth in the Bible and would accept His promises as His pact in the agreement.

For years she had held deep resentments, feeling she had been mistreated. Now she found that she must release to God all personal hurts and also all persons who had hurt her. She was able to do this, for she read: "Dearly beloved, avenge not yourselves, but rather give place unto wrath: for it is written, Vengeance is mine; I will repay, saith the Lord" (Rom. 12:19). A deep consciousness of peace came to her after she asked two persons to forgive her and had written letters to the same effect. This helped her to cleanse her heart of all the malice, resentment, and feelings of injury she had harbored.

Searching the scriptures she compiled a notebook of promises which she called her prescription for healing. These were medicine for the mind, to heal attitudes and feelings, for she realized this was the place where healing must begin: "Be ye transformed by the renewing of your mind" (Rom. 12:2).

She was sure that when her thinking was right healing would reach her body. A new respect for the body came to her as she read: "Know ye not that your body is the temple of the Holy Ghost" (I Cor. 6:19). She asked the Holy Spirit to come and make her body His dwelling place. Perhaps He would if she did as the Holy Word further advised: ". . . present your bodies a living sacrifice, holy, acceptable unto God, which is your reasonable service" (Rom. 12:1).

It was difficult for Rose to maintain a cheerful attitude as she dragged herself from bed, while joints and muscles cried out in pain, but she determined to establish a con-

structive course of action. Clad in robe and slippers she
stood on her back doorstep. Looking at a patch of sky she
said with the Psalmist, "I will lift up mine eyes unto the
hills"; then with his affirmation she went on, "My help
cometh from the Lord, which made heaven and earth"
(Ps. 121:1). Calmly she affirmed, "This is the day that the
Lord hath made"; I will "rejoice and be glad in it"
(Ps. 118:24). Drawing deep breaths she filled her lungs
with fresh air, while remembering that in the New Testament the words *breath* and *spirit* often have the same
meaning. Thinking of the breath which God breathed into
man when he became a living soul, Rose breathed more
deeply. Slowly her body began to respond to the supply of
oxygen it was using, and soon she was ready to shower and
dress.

To get God's promises fixed in her subconscious mind,
Rose placed her book of promises on the kitchen table.
She winced as she reached for the coffee percolator. How
she wanted to be free of stiffness and pain. Quickly she
read: ". . . where the Spirit of the Lord is, there is liberty"
(II Cor. 3:17).

After measuring water into the percolator, she read,
"Verily, verily, I say unto you, Whatsoever ye shall ask the
Father in my name, he will give it you . . . ask, and ye shall
receive, that your joy may be full" (Jn. 16:24). "And all
things, whatsoever ye shall ask in prayer, believing, ye shall
receive" (Matt. 21:22). "For every one that asketh re-
ceiveth; and he that seeketh findeth; and to him that knock-
eth it shall be opened" (Matt. 7:8).

Breaking an egg in the skillet, she glanced at her notebook and read: "Fear not . . . it is your Father's good
pleasure to give you the kingdom" (Lk. 12:32).

Opening the refrigerator Rose quoted, "If ye then, being

evil, know how to give good gifts unto your children, how much more shall your Father which is in heaven give good gifts to them that ask him" (Matt. 7:11).

Buttering toast, she sang softly the phrase she so often had read, "Ye shall know the truth, and the truth shall make you free" (Jn. 8:32).

What is truth, her mind questioned. "I am the way the truth and the life," Jesus' words seemed to answer.

As Rose bowed her head in silent grace a sense of Divine Presence enfolded her. It seemed as if a voice spoke to her heart, saying, "Lo, I am with you alway, even unto the end of the world" (Matt. 28:20).

"I am the Lord that healeth thee" (Ex. 15:26) became an affirmation with every bite. Again and again Rose repeated it until this truth went past her lips, past her conscious thinking, and became an accepted fact in her subconscious mind. Here is the seat of the emotions and here truth must take root before it can become effective. "I am the Lord that healeth thee" she affirmed, then "Lo, I am with you alway," she said again and again. "Always. That is today; right now. God heals me. Now." This became a refrain that sang in her heart. She made the ancient words her own, in an up-to-the-minute paraphrase:

> *I* am with you always,
> I *am* with you always,
> I am with *you* always,
> I am with you *always.*
> I am *Truth,* I am *Life.*
> *I am* the *Lord* that *healeth you.*

Starting to work with a happy heart after completing her affirmations, Rose was determined to keep her thoughts centered on goodness and to think of things for which she could give thanks. She realized that one mounts higher through praise and gratitude than in any other way. All through the day Rose made an effort to practice that advice of Saint Paul: ". . . whatsoever things are true, whatsoever things are honest, whatsoever things are just, whatsoever things are pure, whatsoever things are lovely, whatsoever things are of good report; if there be any virtue, and if there be any praise, think on these things . . . and the God of peace shall be with you" (Phil. 4:8, 9).

When evening came and darkness fell around, Mrs. Allen recalled the words of assurance, "What time I am afraid, I will trust in thee" (Ps. 56:3), and ". . . perfect love casteth out fear" (I Jn. 4:18). So she overcame the eerie feeling that sometimes comes to those who live alone. Fear no longer seemed to lurk in the streets. "God is love" (I Jn. 4:8) embraced her like a mother's arms.

Rose prepared for bed, then heated a cup of milk. While she drank it she said: "I will both lay me down in peace, and sleep: for thou, Lord, only makest me dwell in safety" (Ps. 4:8).

Rose Allen was not healed in a day, a week, or a month, but I can assure you she grew progressively better both in mind and body until she was completely well.

"Yes," she later said with a laugh, "I was healed by saturating my mind with God's promises as I cooked and ate food. I was nourished by God's promises, for I believed they were true."

X

THROUGH FAITH—
THE VICTORY

Genevieve Parkhurst:

It is my happy privilege to share the remarkable story of faith, persistence, and victory that was attained by Miss Edith Leonard, assisted by her friend, Miss Dorothy Van-Deman. Many persons say a prayer hoping some healing may result; but when none is immediately evidenced, they give up easily and make no further effort toward strengthening their faith or clearing their lives of attitudes that may be blocking their healing. Here is a story that surely will open realms of enlightenment and hope to all who read it. Rarely have I known of such faith, such sustained perseverance, such a perfect healing.

Miss Leonard wrote:

The suitcases were being packed, the nose of our green Chrysler Newport was fairly quivering in readiness to be off, and the gypsy corpuscles were surging through Dottie's and my blood streams in anticipation of the extended trip ahead throughout the United States and Canada.

Through retirement in July, 1964, I had "left the life I loved for greater life," to paraphrase Thomas Wolfe. Dottie, my beloved friend, colleague, and general teammate of many years, who was far below the retirement age, had also reoriented her life to the thought of new horizons as we made plans to travel while continuing our writing program. We were going to redirect our creative forces from college texts to children's stories. Up to this time our lives had been lived in a fairly narrow orbit, and we were exhilarated and challenged as we anticipated new worlds to encompass. We were determined that our liberation would bring a glorious state of weightlessness in which we would be free from all pressures and deadlines and have the opportunity to do the many types of things we had been forced to neglect for so long.

Our hearts were in the Rocky Mountains, the forests of Maine, and other beauty areas, but our bodies seemed to be "bound in shallows and miseries" here at home as we made a desperate effort to get uncluttered from all the impedimenta that had enslaved us for many years while we were professors at the University. We were finding to our dismay that a habit of accumulation that has been embedded for more than half a century is fearful, painful, and frustrating!

Then on February 22, 1965, withort warning, we had to put into practical application Glenn Clark's sixth point in *The Divine Plan:* "My disappointments become His appointments." It was with a thankful heart and a deep sense of security that I was at home near my own doctors when, in the midst of assorting our numerous accouterments, I was seized with intense pain and rushed to the hospital. After the trouble was diagnosed as a kidney stone and removed by the surgeon, I was in due time released and for a short while in excellent health, and plans continued for our travels.

In early April, however, I developed excruciating headaches, extreme equilibrium imbalance, and facial and tongue numbness. I was so dizzy I could not stand alone and needed support on both sides in order to walk. The local doctors diagnosed the difficulty as a brain tumor, and I was sent to undergo a battery of agonizing tests by specialists in the field who were equipped with delicate instruments sensitive enough to register the physical source of the trouble.

The series of tests, one where I was stood on my head strapped to a table for four and one-half hours, verified the brain tumor, and drastic surgery was scheduled for the last week in November of 1965. This was to be in two stages of from eight to ten hours each, provided I lived through the first operation.

The specialists were frank in reporting on their findings and explained that serious surgery was imperative and might itself prove fatal, but the tumor would definitely prove so if it were not removed. If I did survive, I might be deaf, blind or have facial distortions and paralysis, or all of these.

Dottie and I were completely stunned and our world seemed to collapse, but our zest for living only became intensified. So we went on in the spirit of a long favorite and oft-repeated quotation from Victor Hugo:

> Like the bird, who
> Halting in his flight
> On limb too slight
> Feels it give way beneath him,
> Yet sings
>   Knowing he has wings.[1]

---

[1] This translation of the Victor Hugo poem appears in the May Hill Arbuthnot Anthology entitled *Time for Poetry,* published by Scott, Foresman and Co., 1961 ed.

When we returned home from the tests, I was completely devasted. The headache was even more difficult to endure, and the rapid and constant pounding pulse beating through the ears, front and back of the head and chest, together with the relentless dizziness, was almost unbearable. The thumping and pounding became so severe that I felt I really might lose my mind. Dottie called the local doctor, who said this and other extreme symptoms were to be expected, and all that could be done for relief was to keep me under sedation. I decided to try to fight it through without medication, because I had in the past been allergic to most pain-reducing drugs and I did not want to wear out the effectiveness of any I might be able to tolerate. As the night wore on it looked as if it would be one of endless torture.

During my intense suffering that long night, I searched my soul and discovered that while I had always considered myself a Christian and had been surrounded by spiritual influences all of my life, I held some strong resentments, antagonisms, and other un-Christlike attitudes.

Is is unfortunate that it seems to take a major impending calamity to bring some of us to a realization that while we have a strong spiritual leaning and consider ourselves true Christians, "our souls," as Starr Daily says, "may be in an arrested state." Perhaps my spiritual forces had been in this passive stage far too long and I needed to become reattuned to God's Infinite Love, Wisdom and Power.

As I talked with my Maker He seemed to lay His hands on me and I had a profoundly shaking rebirth. There was a sudden feeling of expansion, when everything seemed to combine to express a higher level of being, and, for a brief time, I seemed almost to contact the soul of eternity and the eternity of the soul as I released myself completely to God and prayed fervently for forgiveness of all my sins, while wholeheartedly and openly forgiving everyone who had ever trampled on my life or transgressed against me. I found that to forgive myself of my own offenses was the hardest of all, but in that moment when I finally did this, I was filled with love for all humanity, and I saw only the good in all mankind.

I sent universal love out and saluted the divinity within each human soul. I released all tensions, cast out fear, worry, doubt, selfishness, and resentments, and all the other undesirable entities, and prayed that only essences of a worthy nature be swept into my soul, heart, and mind. I gave myself utterly over to God and became quiet and ready to accept His guidance. Much as I wanted to live, I finally reached the point where I could honestly surrender my life, will, and desires to the indwelling Christ and say, "Father, here I am. Take me if you want me."

This was not just a philosophical meditation for several hours during a night of torturous suffering, but a continuous experience that has given Dottie and me a really new life and made us like new people in a new world.

I stopped seeing the problem as it was and visualized it as God would have it. I saw myself radiant, buoyant, healthy, walking straight, a perfect child of God, completely whole in body, mind, and soul, as my Heavenly Father had created me. I knew that He never intended me or anyone else to be ill, and I felt His Divine Love and Healing Power surging through me.

Meditation and communion in solitude with my God went on until exactly 2:30 A.M. when suddenly the violent thumping stopped, the terrific headache and dizziness ceased, and a sense of Peace such as I had never known before came over me. At that moment I experienced the full meaning of "the peace that passeth understanding."

I got up out of bed and walked across the room, straight as an arrow. This was the first time in six months that I had gone even a yard without support and been free from severe suffering.

I wakened Dottie and we spent the rest of the night in prayer, song, and thanksgiving. With this start we began a fervent seeking of Spiritual Healing for me. We went more deeply into prayer, meditation, contemplation, study, and soul searching, and our awareness of the spirit of love, trust, and thanksgiving transcended all we had ever perceived or encountered up to that time. We became increasingly aware of how much we are on the receiving side. We knew, however, that God can only give us His blessings and strength as we are willing to reach for them and, at the same time, to pay the price of making His gifts a part of ourselves.

We temporarily discontinued our newspaper and other secular reading in order to keep our environment on the highest spiritual plane and to give more time to the Bible and all types of books on spiritual growth, which now became our constant companions. Many of the Biblical characters took on living personalities.

We saturated ourselves with the splendor of God's wonders: sunrises, sunsets, the close stars, the drifting moon and yellow sunlight filtering through the trees. Each for us had a new brilliance.

Impressive, familiar poems, music, color and design in all its varied forms brought a deeper response in us and their loveliness seemed to flow through us like a symphony. We went about our daily tasks with a constant song in our hearts. Among our favorites still are "Breathe on me, Breath of God," "Still, still with Thee," "Dear Lord and Father of mankind," and "Standing on the Promises."

We were amazed to discover that there are over 30,000 promises in the Bible. One of the most helpful to us is found in Mark 11:24, "Therefore, I say unto you, What things soever ye desire, when ye pray, believe that ye receive them, and ye shall have them." Another much loved one: "I have heard thy prayer, I have seen thy tears: behold, I will heal thee" (II Kgs. 20:5). Another favorite, from John 15:7: "If you abide in me, and my words abide in you, ask whatever you will, and it shall be done for you" (R.S.V.). And from Psalm 37:5: "Commit thy way unto the Lord; trust also in Him; and he shall bring it to pass."

Friends of practically every Christian faith undergirded us with their prayers, and we sought counsel and guidance from various sources—our own and many other church groups, Prayer and Healing Centers, and more advanced and trained persons who are channels for God's Healing Forces.

We knew, however, that others, no matter how powerful their spiritual vitality, could not lift me out of my problem! I had to be an active participant in discovering the truth that healing must come from within me, myself. As Norman Vincent Peale says, "The great breakthrough in anything comes when you work at it and practice it." Dottie and I felt like the young lad who was running away from a bear, and prayed, "I'll pick up my feet, God, if you'll put them down." This kind of teamwork is what it takes. God will do His part if we will but do ours.

So while healing is really as natural as breathing if we give and receive in the perfect joy and freedom with which God gives us His Universe, none of *us* can heal, no matter how many are gathered with one purpose; this is *God's* glory and His alone. We constantly rejoiced that our Heavenly Father does not demand perfection of living before He enters into us with His Healing Love, Light, and Power.

During the next few weeks there were regressions and improvements with intermittent return of the intense pain.

The prolonged, exacting, and agonizing November tests gave evidence that the pressure of growth was still present and surgery was imperative. The doctors said the tumor would not dissolve or in any other way disappear; but at my earnest pleadings for extended time to complete some "unfinished symphonies," the surgeons agreed to advance the dates for the operations to the first and second weeks in January.

Because our *belief* had changed to *faith,* and our faith to *knowing* that spiritual healing was taking place, I later pleaded for a second and then a third postponement of the surgery. Perhaps the doctors thought I was going to die, and, knowing I was a professional person interested in writing, they may have reasoned if it meant so much to me to try to leave some "footprints on the sands of time," why not humor me.

Dottie and I knew in our hearts that perfect and permanent healing would be mine in God's own time and in His own way, according to His Providential Plan. Any impatience over delay or any doubts creeping in we knew would only prevent the full and complete healing.

So it was with confidence and singing in our hearts and voices that I reported for pre-operative tests on March 7, 1966. We had high expectations that they would prove I was restored and made whole. We accepted the perfection with radiant acquiescence and gave thanks and praise to our Heavenly Father for it.

However, the specialists said when they checked me that it would be incredible for a tumor such as mine to go away, and they prepared to proceed with the jugular vein X-rays to give more definite information to help with the surgery. Because of our deep conviction that the Great Physician of all would remove the tumor, the doctors finally but reluctantly responded to my pleas for a repeat of the October and November tests, plus the jugular venogram, provided the laboratory were available, which it proved to be, as Dottie and I knew it would.

I was admitted to the Hospital early the next morning as a pre-operative patient. During the tests throughout those two days Dottie and I prayed unceasingly, and the impact of these prayers and those of friends and Prayer Groups throughout the United States resulted in my actually feeling the tumor disappear during the pantopaque test. God found His own beautiful way and His own perfect timing to perform the miracle.

The test results, compared with the X-rays taken in October and November, showed that area of my head all cleared up and filled in. The condition was as different as if the earlier and later X-rays had been taken on two separate skulls.

The healing was verified the next day before the scheduled hour for the surgery when three physicians and five nurses came into my room and the chief surgeon said, "You do not now have a tumor, but we want to check you again in three months."

Three months to the day, June 7, 1966, I reported back to the specialists and they gave me a permanent release.

On September 7, six months from the date of the *great experience,* I was given a thorough physical check-up by the local doctors, one of whom said, "When you were here last fall you said you were seeking a miraculous healing. I could not accept your faith at that time, but it looks as if that is exactly what you received—a miraculous healing. This is the only explanation I can give for your present excellent health."

Dottie and I are devoutly thankful to our Heavenly Father, and there is a constant song in our hearts for my Spiritual Healing through faith and prayer. Neither of us will ever be the same again for no healing is complete until it takes place in the whole being—spirit and mind as well as body. It is all so beautiful and glorious that our finite minds can scarcely perceive it, but our hearts and souls rejoice in the complete miracle. Now it is our souls' sincere desire to be ambassadors for Christ and do our bit to minister to the human needs around us, wherever He may lead.

Of all the blessings associated with this *great experience,* one of the most heart-warming is the radiant response from others who seek the power of God's healing love. Vera Wilson, on hearing our testimony, shared the poem that came to her while meditating on Glenn Clark's *The Divine Plan*. Her inspired words are a perfect embodiment of our own highest aspirations. With her we say:

> There is a longing deep within
>   To find God's plan for me
> To be the shining, radiant soul
>   That I was meant to be.
> There is a call, the call of Christ
>   To be His hands and feet
> To speak the words and see his face
>   In every soul I meet.
>
> There is a thirsting in my soul
>   For living water, free
> To cleanse within and flow without

His channel pure to be
Bringing the healing power of Christ
    To body, mind and soul
The power of His redeeming love
    That makes the wounded whole.

There is an urgency within
    To share the Christian way
To spread throughout the world the news
    That Jesus lives today.
He lives and moves in wondrous ways
    His power to impart
Through every soul who offers Him
    A yielding, contrite heart.

There is a hunger in my heart
    That I can never fill
Until I give myself to God
    To do His holy will—
Not just my talents, just my time
    Nor yet the tithes I give
But all I have, and all I am
    That He, through me, might live.

XI

THE WILL TO LIVE

THE WILL TO LIVE is a strong factor in healing. Sometimes a person who seems on the road to recovery will die, while one who has everything against him will make a remarkable recovery. Very often the difference is that the one who recovers has a determination to live. When one has a sense of destiny, a feeling that he has a specific work to do or mission to fulfill, he will rally as to a bugle call. On the other hand, when an ill person feels that life has passed him by, that there is nothing to live for, it often is difficult to get him to make a fight for life. This points out the necessity of having a goal in life and of feeling needed.

Scott Winters lay in a Veterans' Tuberculosis Hospital, surrounded by the dying, knowing he might be the next to be carried out, and not caring if he was. What had he to live for? He was sick with an "incurable" disease and there was no one to care. His wife and son had been riding with his parents when a drunken driver ran head-on into their car and killed them all. They were all of Scott's relatives except one sister who was half a world away.

"Maybe this will waken hope in you," the Gray Lady

107

said smiling as she laid a magazine beside Scott's bed. "There is nothing like a seed catalogue to give a fellow spring fever."

Listlessly Scott picked up the magazine and looked at the brightly colored pictures of blooming flowers and luscious vegetables. He smiled in spite of himself. "How the fellows that put out these catalogues accentuated the positive!" he thought. He dropped the thin booklet, but his mind took hold of something, as memory responded to suggestion.

"A garden," Scott mused. What wouldn't he give to raise a garden. In fancy, he was a boy walking in his mother's garden, picking English peas, hulling them in his hand, and eating the milky-sweet fruit. Peas never tasted as good when cooked as they did when he munched them raw. This was a secretive act, like bursting a watermelon in the patch and gouging out the heart with his pocket knife. Scott smiled, remembering. Then his awakened mind raced on, recalling happy days of his boyhood on a farm.

Now he studied the seed catalogue carefully. He would make a garden! That was what he would do! That was what he wanted to do. Plans began to form. His friends, Fred and Ellen Hartley, had stood by him throughout the years. They had been to see him and a few days ago Fred had mentioned that he had purchased a farm which joined his land; the former owners had moved from it leaving the house vacant. Maybe Fred would be a good Samaritan and help him get out of the hospital into the sunshine and live again. He would ask Fred to take him to this house now that spring was in the air, and he would plant a garden. That was what he would do. With this determination new life began to stir in Scott Winters' body.

It took some doing to secure a release from the hospital,

but Fred agreed to be responsible for Scott, and finally he was bundled in blankets and placed in the back seat of Fred's car. The ride was exhausting, but Scott clung to every ounce of strength he had so as not to frighten Fred and Ellen for fear they might take him back to the hospital. He was going to a farm! He would raise a garden and eat fresh peas. He would. This he would do.

Scott insisted he should occupy the vacant house on the farm. Ellen made up a bed in it for him and Fred slept on a cot in an adjoining room. At times during the night he drifted off into unconsciousness deeper than sleep, but he pulled himself back to rationality with thoughts of his garden and this, his house, a farm, life, his dog, the meadow, the woods, his mother in the kitchen, father coming in from the fields. Scott slept, a peaceful sleep such as he had not known in weeks.

The next day, bundled in blankets, Scott lay on a cot in the warm sunshine. Since he had arrived late in the evening, he had not realized the place was so beautiful, so filled with spring flowers. Near the house there was an apple tree, glorious with blossoms, softly pink and fragrant. Lilac bushes were in full bloom beside the porch. A forsythia glowed, a yellow ball in the sunshine, and tulips blossomed beside the front walk. "The people who had lived here must have loved this place," Scott thought, and wondered why they had sold it.

Interest wakened in him in succeeding days as he watched Fred plow and harrow the garden plot. Fred's son, Kennie, made rows across the freshly turned loam as Scott directed and planted seeds. Soon there were lettuce, radishes, carrots, and beets growing, while newly set onions showed rows of green in the brown soil. Later he would put out peas, beans, sweet corn, and tomatoes. What he couldn't eat he would give away, Scott thought. He knew the value of fresh vegetables in restoring health. Guess the Lord had supplied about all a fellow needed to keep well in giving him fresh air, sunshine, clean water, and the vegetation of the earth, Scott mused. The food Ellen brought tasted good those evenings. Scott knew he was getting well.

Shag, a beautiful collie dog, usually came with Kennie. He would follow his young master home, then return to sit beside Scott, looking into his face understandingly as if he had found a kindred spirit. Perhaps this dog's ancestors had shared life with him on a farm years ago, Scott soliloquized. If the dog had no such memories the man relived many, as in spirit he roved the fields, his dog beside him. They chased rabbits which outran them, rolled in lush grass, and dreamed in cool shadows beneath friendly trees. Shag's nose on his hand brought Scott back to reality.

The sun grew warm. Rows of green stretched across his garden. Each day Scott walked as far as he could, rested, and returned to his chair beneath the apple tree. He was now cooking his own meals.

One day as Scott was feeling the need of human companionship, Martin Slater came by and stopped under the apple tree where Scott was sitting. Friendly and genial, the elderly man spoke of the people who had recently moved from this farm and of his pleasure at seeing someone living here again.

"Deserted houses are sad," he said, "especially farm houses. They do not stand anonymously as a house in the city does; they are surrounded by trees and shrubs and blooming things that women love. They have houses to shelter chickens and machinery. Farm houses are built to grow in, and everything around them becomes a part of the people who live there." The sun-tanned face of Scott's visitor was pensive as he went on, "Yes, a deserted farm house is like a mother who has raised a family and then is pushed out and left in the cold." Martin continued, "I'm mighty glad to see you here," and nodded his head approvingly. "You will become attached to this place. It's been lived in. There is a feel to a place that's been lived in."

"I believe you are right," Scott agreed. "There is a feel to a place that has been lived in." Scott paused, then smiled and finished, "Lived in and loved. I guess anything that has been loved has a feel about it."

"I guess love is what we die for the want of," Martin went on. "Things are mighty convenient to have but we need folks. We need folks to love and to care whether we live or die. Yes, we need folks." Martin affirmd meditatively as he picked up a stick and began to whittle.

Scott wondered how much this neighbor knew about him.

"Mighty fine folks around here," Martin said. "Good people, kind and considerate. The kind of people who will help a neighbor any time he needs it. Will Davis broke his leg and the men of the community went in and harvested his crops. Didn't let a grain go to waste. Folks here are like that."

"That's good," Scott said softly.

Martin resumed his whittling. For some minutes nothing was said, then he glanced sidewise and went on. "Neighborhoods like this are scarce these days. People move to the cities. Schools are consolidated, the children carried in buses to town, the community churches are largely gone so the people aren't brought together in neighborly fellowship as they used to be." Martin looked up from his whittling, "But this place is the exception. We still have our church service and our community sings and sociables. The city hasn't squeezed the life out of us—yet."

"That's good," Scott offered.

"We'll be mighty glad to have you join us whenever you feel like it. Mighty glad to have you," Martin rose to go.

"Come again," Scott smiled—a real smile that he felt.

"I'll do that." Martin's eyes crinkled. "By the way, do you play checkers? I have a lot of time on my hands. I live with my son and his family. The chickens are my project. They give me something to do, to be responsible for and interested in. I'll come in my pickup and take you to see my chickens."

"I would like to see them," Scott agreed. "Next time you come bring your checkers and we can have a game."

Not only did the two men play checkers, they rode into town to buy groceries and do errands for Martin's son, who was busy in the fields. At Martin's insistence Scott went with him to the little country church. Fred and Ellen were there and were delighted to see him. He found here a friendliness he did not know existed. He was accepted as if he belonged to these people. He prayed with them, worshipped with them, and into his heart came the warm consciousness of God which he once had known but had lost. Scott Winters was finding healing deeper than the need of his body.

Evenings when Fred would come over the two men talked together and after he had gone Scott would sit looking into the sky. The stars were brightest when the moon was dark, and when the moon was full, it spread a silver gauze over everything about the place, softening harsh lines and creating beauty out of ugliness. Scott felt a kinship with all things, a part of everything, cosmic consciousness some might say. The realization came that he who is at peace with God is at home in all the universe.

Scott had been a nominal Christian; that is, he had a

wholesome respect for the Almighty, but now he had come to know Him, real and near, yes, even friendly. With the ancient Psalmist he said again and again, "The heavens declare the glory of God; and the firmament sheweth his handywork. Day unto day uttereth speech, and night unto night sheweth knowledge" (Ps. 19: 1, 2). "O Lord our Lord, how excellent is thy name in all the earth! . . . When I consider thy heavens, the work of thy fingers, the moon and the stars, which thou hast ordained; What is man, that thou art mindful of him? and the son of man, that thou visitest him?" (Psalm 8:1, 3, 4).

Finding God, Scott found himself, and life surged into his body. Reading how the great botanist and scientist, George Washington Carver, lived in the fields and woods until the quietness of nature became his, Scott began to sense such peace as he walked in the sunshine among grasses and wild flowers. He looked with new interest upon all growing things as he thought how Doctor Carver had found food value and medicinal uses for many plants which were called weeds. As he studied the life of Dr. Albert Schweitzer, Scott began to understand the meaning of his expression, "reverence for life," and felt a closeness to every living thing.

It seemed to Scott that his life matured and his understanding expanded as he hoed in his garden and lay, dressed in light shorts and moccasins, his skin baking a deep brown in the sunshine. Firm flesh covered his frame as he continued to eat his garden produce. Sitting cross-legged beneath his apple tree, his back against its trunk, he ate bowls of lettuce with a bit of lemon juice. He had forgotten how good deep red tomatoes ripened on the vine could taste, and he enjoyed sweet corn at its best—dropped into boiling water within minutes after being taken from the stalk, cooked three minutes or long enough to set the milk in the grains, and spread with country butter. Scott's garden fulfilled all his hopes.

Relaxing on the ground, Scott felt he knew why people were nervous, and thought they needed alcohol as a stimulant. Like electric wires people need to be grounded. Housed in apartments, never getting their feet on the ground or touching the earth, they become high strung and flighty.

Scott discarded his cot and lay each day on the warm ground. Strength and healing came into him from it. "The earth is the mother of our bodies and the Divine Spirit father of our immortal souls," he mused, "and we need the caress of both." Perhaps men vaguely sense this. Maybe that is why they seek the outdoors, walk over a golf course, go fishing, tramp over fields with a gun, and drive, drive, drive, anywhere so long as it is into the open air.

By the time frost was in the air Scott was a healthy man. His problem now was to leave the quiet country and go back to the hurried life of the city, where men drink to pep themselves up, and drink to quiet themselves down, then drive high-powered automobiles which become weapons of death; where women suffer nervous prostration and men succumb to heart attacks. It would be easier to stay on in this house. Fred would allow him to spend the winter here. Scott mulled over the possibility. No, he decided, this would be evading responsibility. He must live again. He must return to the work he was trained to do. He must live among people. Martin was right. We need people if we are to be happy. But could he fit into the fevered life he had tried to escape?

He had found healing, but now he realized that health requires more than fresh air, sunshine, water, and the vegetation of the earth. To be really healthy one also needs companionship and love. One can't enjoy normal health without these; the love of people in work and play, in love and worship. And one needs a worthwhile work to do. He also needs the love of God to fulfill life. Perhaps God would help him now in making his decision.

With a prayer for guidance Scott studied his New Testament. As he looked at the page before him these words of Jesus gave him the answer: "These things I have spoken unto you, that in me ye might have peace. In the world ye shall have tribulation: but be of good cheer; I have overcome the world" (Jn. 16:33).

XII

I WALKED, I RAN,
I FLOATED

Faith has been likened to the confidence of a child, who when told by his father to jump from a high ladder into his outstretched arms, makes a leap through the air, confident of being caught. Such a leap of faith was taken by the person whose story follows. She held no reservations, expressed no doubts, but leaped into the arms of our Divine Father, with utter abandon of self and complete reliance in God. Since the healing which took place seven years ago, my friend has enjoyed abundant health. We now share with you this beautiful experience.

In the late June sunshine, the buildings on the tree-shaded University Campus brooded in dignified silence: wise mothers whose elder children had gone forth, diplomas in hand, to meet life. Now a group of various ages was gathering from many states. During the next eight days some three hundred persons would join in happy fellowship and sharing while seeking wholeness of body, mind, and spirit. The Camps Farthest Out, as their founder,

Glenn Clark, described them, are a cross between the almost forgotten Camp Meeting and the Chautauqua, affording both intellectual and spiritual development, with emphasis upon the reality of prayer as related to the problems of everyday life.

"Professor Farnsworth wishes to see you," I was told as soon as I entered the registration building.

"Who is Professor Farnsworth?" I asked.

"Mrs. Angela Farnsworth is a teacher here. She wants to see you as soon as possible, preferably before the Camp sessions begin," came the answer.

Taken to a small room off the dining room, I waited, wondering why a professor of this University wished to see me.

I looked up. A beautiful woman was standing at the door. Tall and stately with classic features, she was a picture of patrician dignity.

"You are Mrs. Parkhurst," she said as she extended her hand. "I have been counting the days and hours until you would be here. It is my feet," she said as we were seated. "Will you pray for them?"

Moving to a hassock in front of Mrs. Farnsworth I lifted her feet to my lap and removed shoes with the highest heels I had ever seen. The feet seemed solid, unmoving in the joints, the arches rigid, the toes drawn toward the heels.

"How long have you had this trouble?" I asked, gently massaging the rigid feet.

"All my life it seems. I was very ill when I was eight months old. The doctor then thought I had scarlet fever. Later an orthopedic surgeon said I must have had a mild case of poliomyelitis. My feet did not give me much trouble until I was in High School, although I would fall up stairs, down stairs and on the level. In High School I had to give up basketball. My movements showed and as my feet drew out of shape my parents took me to numerous doctors. But I kept going."

"Were the doctors able to help you?" I asked.

"No. They would say, 'If you had come sooner.' That was cold comfort. So I just wore higher and higher heels." Mrs. Farnsworth smiled. "When I married, my husband tried to find help for me. My feet were so deformed that I could not take one step without five-inch heels, not even in the night to see if the babies were covered. I would walk on the sides of my feet when no one was looking." A wry laugh escaped the tense lips. "Finally I did have surgery. The surgeons spliced and lengthened the drawn tendons six inches. I lay for months without walking. That was twenty years ago. When I was up, again my feet began to draw. Later my doctor son sent me to a noted orthopedic surgeon, but my uncle doctor advised against further surgery and said that as long as I possibly could get around, I should do that regardless of the pain.

"But every step has been like walking on hot coals, as the bones of the metatarsus slip out of their sockets and back with each step while I steel myself against showing pain."

I sat, gently rubbing the rigid feet, while I prayed silently.

"A friend loaned me your book, *Healing and Wholeness*," [1] Mrs. Farnsworth went on. "It gave me hope, so here I am. It is either divine healing or a wheel chair."

A flood of compassion washed over me. Like waves that sweep one from the shore into the ocean, this divine love seemed to lift and carry us together into a vast, unbounded,

---

[1] Macalaster Park Publishing Co., Saint Paul, Minnesota, and Arthur James, Ltd., England.

spiritual reality beyond the reaches of material being. A light, a power beyond mortal understanding drew us together and lifted us beyond ourselves. Tears flowed unchecked, for the Holy Spirit was in possession. I rubbed the legs, the knees, and, dropping beside Mrs. Farnsworth's chair, began rubbing her lower spine and hips, holding my hands on areas where they were guided, as power like electricity flowed through them. This was not I but the Holy Spirit who worked through me. As Jesus said, "Of myself I can do nothing. It is the Father who doeth the work" (*cf*. Jn. 5:17ff), so, the Spirit ministered.

When the power abated, we sat in silence. Finally I said, "Relax. Rest awhile." So we leaned back in our chairs and were still. Fifteen minutes passed. Then Mrs. Farnsworth put on her shoes. When she stood up, a look of wonder spread over her face.

"It doesn't hurt!" The words were awed. "I can't believe it. There is no pain."

"Sit down," I said. "Let us talk a bit. The healing has begun. Now you must see that it goes on to completion."

"How can I do that?"

"Have you seen fireflies over a meadow at night?" I asked.

"Yes."

"You know your blood circulates, carrying oxygen to every part of your body. The body is renewed by the blood stream. As you lie on your bed, think of God's healing light going through your body; not as a blaze of light, but as millions of tiny sparks like fireflies circulating in your blood with the red and white corpuscles. The red blood cells nourish, the white corpuscles cleanse, the sparks of divine light heal. Lie still and make a picture in your mind of this taking place in your body. Focus your thought on the area of your body that needs healing and see, in your mind's eye, these sparks of light gathering around this sore spot, reviving, renewing, and healing. Be still as the treatment goes on. Be still, receive, and give thanks. Now, it would be well if you could rest, perhaps sleep."

At home Mrs. Farnsworth slept. And it was in sleep that a miracle took place. When she awakened, her stiff, deformed feet were transformed. They had become soft, supple, and moved in every joint. They were perfectly healed and restored to normal. She came back to the University wearing moccasins, for she did not have a pair of shoes she could wear because her feet were longer since they had become normal.

She stood at the dining room door, taking tickets from the three hundred campers who went past, glowing with joy, and radiating this happiness to all who entered the room. Later she shared the experience of her healing at one of our meetings.

That summer Mrs. Farnsworth took a tour through Canada with a group and walked everywhere the others did without discomfort.

Now comes a part of this story which is vital to everyone who has received a healing through prayer. While Mrs. Farnsworth was free of pain all summer while she was away from her work happily sightseeing, when she returned to the classroom and once more found herself under the stress and tension there, her feet began to hurt. Tension and stress, as Dr. Selye points out, began to have a telling effect.

What was she to do? She was not able of herself to generate sufficient divine power to stop the pain. But she knew the power was available. She had felt it and she knew the group which had brought the Camp to the University. She telephoned the Chairman of the Camp Council Ring and asked them to pray for her. They met for this purpose. She joined them. Once more all pain left her feet and it has never returned.

Later Mrs. Farnsworth visited in my home. As she sat in my living room. I dropped on the floor at her feet and, taking off her low-heeled shoes, held her beautiful, supple feet in my hands, as gratitude rose to God like incense.

Since that time Mrs. Farnsworth has been employed in Egypt and Turkey as a guide to show tourists the sights. Although constantly on her feet, they have held up through days of ceaseless walking.

Of her experience there Mrs. Farnsworth has said: "You cannot imagine the thousands of kilometers I have walked over rough ground, rock-piled ruins, up high mountains to Crusaders Castles, quite literally pulling myself up some of the steep slopes. Imagine! Me without pain, who, but for the Grace of God, would have been in a wheel chair. And this is interesting—ever since my healing, when I get 'off the beam,' whether I realize it or not, my feet tell me. They begin to hurt in the same old way, until I correct my error."

Listening intently then to Professor Farnsworth's testimony, my heart was stilled. I wondered if pain in our bodies is a signal from God that we have drifted off the beam.

If you feel the need for more strength in your prayer for the victory of physical release, find a group who have power in prayer, tell them your need, and release your faith anew as they pray for you. Jesus said, "For where two or three are gathered together in my name, there am I in the midst of them" (Matt. 18:20). Hold fast His word as your promise of renewal.

XIII

HEALING THROUGH THE EUCHARIST

THE CROSS IS AN EMBLEM of the Christian faith, and the sacrament of the Lord's Supper is an affirmation of His presence in His Church. Jesus' promise to be with His followers always is realized in His Spiritual Presence. Those who believe Him receive the emblems of His shed blood and broken body in remembrance of Him.

There is no magic in these elements. They will be to the unbelieving only bread and wine, or grape juice. But they are an outward sign of an inward grace, provide a psychological aid in inspiring faith, and thus enable the communicant to become conscious of God's presence. They are a channel through which the power of God can flow. Those who accept them as such usually are blessed. So many healings have occurred through this sacrament that many persons accept it as having healing power. For them, it is a means of receiving into their lives a power greater than their own and of linking their lives with the life of the Infinite. By faith, God has been able to transform them in body, mind, and spirit.

In literature wine symbolized spirit. So the wine of the sacrament may be a symbol of the Spirit of Christ. The bread which represents His body may also have reference to ours. As we partake of the bread we may think that He is saying to us, "Since I have no physical body, will you carry on in yours the work I began on earth?" As we receive the wine we may hear His call to allow His spirit to fill us. This can be a meaningful purpose for partaking of this Sacrament, and as Christ's Spirit fills every cell of our bodies, they should become like His—whole. Christ's Atonement was also for our healing, for "he was wounded for our transgressions . . . and with his stripes we are healed" (Is. 53:5).

Returning from Europe where my husband and I had gone with a group to study the art of healing through prayer as it is done in many places there, I left the pier in New York and went to Niagara Falls for a speaking engagement. I reached the home of the friend with whom I was to stay while there and had not been in the house over an hour when a telephone call came from Mrs. Peter Dooley, who asked to talk with me.

Soon Mrs. Dooley, whom my friend called Clothilde, arrived. My heart went out to her for her need was evident. Fear was written on her face and registered in her voice. She explained that her fear was for the child she was carrying. Due to an Rh blood factor condition she seemed in danger of losing the baby. She and her husband had one child, their first who was born normally, but since then they had lost two babies. Now, in the sixth month of this fourth child's pre-natal development, Mrs. Dooley's doctor had tested her blood for Rh antibodies in the bloodstream, and the reading had been 28, which he referred to as elevated and said could be damaging. He said the Rh antibody reading might go higher. This was what she feared.

"We want this baby so much," her voice quavered. "Can you do anything to help me?"

As I prayed silently my mind returned to another case almost exactly like this one and to that which resulted in healing for both mother and child. The compassion which flooded my being led me to speak.

"There is something," I began, wondering if Clothilde would think me a fanatic.

"Yes? What is it?" she asked eagerly.

"As I understand such cases," I spoke hesitantly, "the child is sometimes saved by draining off the blood which is in its veins at the time of birth and giving it the blood of a third party."

"Yes, I've been told that," she agreed.

"There is the blood of Christ which we take emblematically in the sacrament of Holy Communion," I told her.

"Would that help?" The question registered amazement.

"It has," I answered. "Are you willing to try it?"

"Could we find a minister who would give us the elements on a week day?" Mrs. Dooley's question was her answer, and a light of hope was in her eyes.

Our hostess telephoned to a friend who gave her the name of an Episcopal priest whom she thought would give us the sacrament. Most graciously he consented and set the time for eight-thirty the next morning.

"One thing more," I inquired of Clothilde. "What will your husband think of our doing this? This is his child, and it is necessary that he be in accord with the prayer."

"Oh, he will be delighted," she beamed. "His mother was a student of Christian Science, and when he was a boy he was taught the reality of healing through prayer."

The following morning, which was a Friday, we three women went to the Episcopal Church whose rector had agreed to see us. Here we were met by a most gracious clergyman who talked with us awhile. After putting on his clerical vestments he gave the elements to the three of us who knelt before the altar. He performed the service of Holy Communion, using all the ritual, with as much reverence as if his sanctuary had been filled with communicants.

Following the service the rector invited us to the rectory, which was next door to the church, where his gracious wife served us coffee and cakes. As we were eating I looked across the room at Clothilde. Her arms, which were bare in a sleeveless dress and had been the color of chalk, were now a rosy pink.

"Oh, my dear," I whispered, "something has happened to your circulation."

"It sure has," she agreed. "I am hot all over."

The following Monday, when Mrs. Dooley's blood test was again taken, the technician brought the doctor the record of a reading of 14. Looking at the chart the doctor called for the last reading. It was brought and showed 28. "Something amiss here," the doctor told the technician, and insisted he had made a mistake. But when the records were checked, it was confirmed that while Mrs. Dooley's blood had indeed tested a reading of "antibodies 28" on Friday, it tested "14" the following Monday. Another test confirmed the later reading.

Through the argument of doctor and technician Mrs. Dooley sat, saying nothing. When she reached home she telephoned me.

"What should I have said?" she asked.

"Wouldn't it have been best to have told them the truth?" I asked.

"Oh, I couldn't." she cried. "The doctor is a Roman Catholic."

"That's great," I responded. "Who would believe more in the power of the Mass than a Roman Catholic? Transubstantiation is a doctrine of his Church which says that during the Eucharist the substances of the bread and wine are changed into the body and blood of Christ. Your doctor will understand what took place in your body during the service as you received the Sacrament."

The doctor did understand. He agreed to watch Mrs. Dooley's condition closely.

Mr. Dooley came with his wife to the retreat at which I was speaking. I was happy to make his acquaintance and learned that he was an elder in the Presbyterian Church and had served as Sunday School Superintendent. About three months later this man's voice rang out as I answered my telephone early one morning.

"I must let you know that we have a fine boy, born this morning." Happiness was in every word as he went on, "He is perfect in every way. There was no sign of jaundice and he needed no blood transfusion."

Of course this baby needed no blood transfusion. He had had one!

This experience was most beautiful in its demonstration of the perfect harmony in which people who love God first of all can work together. Here was a woman of a Presbyterian Church, whose husband was reared by a mother of the Christian Science faith, in the home of a Methodist, receiving the Sacrament from an Episcopal priest for the healing of the blood of the mother and her unborn child, and her doctor, a Roman Catholic, caring for the mother until a perfect child came to birth.

Truly, God is good, as we often sing:

> For the love of God is broader
>   Than the measure of man's mind;
> And the heart of the Eternal
>   Is most wonderfully kind.

XIV

GOD CURES
THE INCURABLE

Genevieve Parkhurst:

Jesus healed persons rather then merely curing diseases. Such persons as are divinely healed often rise to a higher dimension of life than they have known before their healing. It may be that in making a complete consecration of their lives to God as they pray for healing, God is able to push back the horizon of their understanding and allow them to comprehend possibilities which before were undreamed of. Such expanding consciousness often releases innate potentials and brings a joyous abandon to these who are healed and enables them to rise above former limitations as they become effective witnesses to God's power.

Roy Amstutz shares the story of his healing and tells of the fullness of life that has opened before him as God called him from carpenter to clergyman.

Roy Amstutz:
"God heals today even as He healed long ago," the speaker was saying. "The power of Jesus Christ is as great and His presence as real as it was when He walked the hills

of Nazareth and the shores of Galilee." The miracles of healing in the Bible were real, I know, and some people were coming into new life today, but could it happen to me? From childhood there had been a belief in God's power to heal, but for someone who had an "incurable" disease, this seemed a great deal to ask.

My mind skipped back several years as I remembered why I was sitting here in this Methodist Church in Sydney, Ohio, one day in November, 1958. Just a little more than two years before, I had become aware of a numbness in the index finger of my right hand. As the weather grew colder, the numbness spread quickly to the whole hand, then the other, and soon to the feet also. During the cold Ohio winter my hands and feet would feel wooden after only a few minutes' work outside. After about an hour, fingers would turn blue and stiff and remain in this condition even after I was in the warm for several hours; so I finally went to our family doctor in Wooster, Ohio. He quickly diagnosed the trouble as Raynaud's Disease and recommended that I go to the Cleveland Clinic for observation and tests.

After two days of testing, the Clinic doctors confirmed the diagnosis of Raynaud's Disease, telling me that it was a disease of the sympathetic nervous system. When I went into the cold, the nerves would restrict the flow of blood in the circulatory system, and the blood would not circulate freely in my hands and feet. Several kinds of medicine were given me to dilate the arteries, and the maximum dosage of tranquilizers was also given to offset the uncomfortable side effects of the medicine. The only other possibility was a series of prolonged operations cutting the nerves of the sympathetic nervous system. These operations were not recommended, however.

When I returned for further observation, the doctors kept questioning me about the hardness of the skin of my hands. They feared that I might be slipping into scleroderma which is at times a companion to Raynaud's Disease. It was suggested that a warm, dry climate might be desirable.

As the summor wore on plans were laid to go to Tucson, Arizona. I was working at two part-time jobs, helping to operate a small dairy-farming operation and working as a carpenter. Late in August the cows were sold, I quit my carpenter job, and early in September my wife, our three children, and I were Arizona bound. There we rented one-half a furnished duplex and I worked as a carpenter during our stay in Tucson. We called it a working vacation.

Only a part of the sixteen pills had to be taken each day while we were in Tucson. The progression of the disease, however, was constant. Whenever I fell asleep my hands, arms, legs, and feet would "fall asleep" too, and when I awoke, there was a very uncomfortable and upsetting prickling, tingling sensation. The circulation was impaired to the extent that one Sunday morning when I crossed my arms, my hand pressed against a button of my suit coat and left an indentation. Several hours later the imprint was still visible. I don't know how long it stayed.

When my hands were a little cool, my fingers would turn white and flatten out, staying that way for awhile if I pressed my fingers against a surface or picked something up. My skin seemed to be losing its resiliency. I could press and mould the flesh of my fingers into various shapes and the flesh would remain in that shape for some time. Another sign of the progression of the Raynaud's Disease or scleroderma was that I could pick up very hot articles and feel no pain for five or ten seconds. The reaction time was slowing up considerably.

One Sunday evening a psychologist spoke in the church I attended. She spoke of the effects of the mind on the health of the body, and of God's ability to heal man of any and every kind of disease. At the close of the lecture I asked if she felt that wrong thinking played any part in my illness. She pointed out that we are whole beings and that each part—body, mind, and spirit—contributes to our total wholeness.

About a year after the onset of this disease I went to this psychologist for a number of counseling sessions. One of the hurdles that had to be overcome was the belief that perhaps it was God's will that I should be sick. The answer that God never wills anyone to be sick, and the explanation that sickness did not bring glory to God, but that health did, made sense.

Intellectual belief and heart belief, however, are two different things. The seed of hope was planted, but it took some time to mature and bear fruit. To aid my faith in its growing process and to help stimulate new thinking, several books were supplied for reading and a tape for listening. I read the books with some understanding but the tape had a great effect on me. In this tape Genevieve Parkhurst told of her healing of cancer and her subsequent search to become a channel of God's healing power. The tape was played over and over until Mrs. Parkhurst seemed to become a warm personal friend.

Toward the end of May we started back to Ohio. It seemed advisable to attempt to contact Genevieve on our way home, but we learned that she was speaking in the East, so we returned home greatly disappointed because we were unable to see her.

Later in the summer my wife wrote to Genevieve and learned that during the month of November both the Rev.

and Mrs. Parkhurst were to be in Western Ohio, leading a number of prayer conferences. It appeared that a trip to see them would be advisable.

The doctors had said that, medically, there was little they could do. I was becoming very stiff and slow in my movements. Riding in a car left me unable to straighten up for five or ten minutes. There was difficulty thinking and sometimes a sort of numbness when I tried to think. In October the family attended a football game. I wore three or four layers of clothes, among them an insulated suit designed for 20 degrees below zero, plus wool underwear, a wool sweater, a wool shirt, corduroy trousers, a jacket, insulated mittens, and a stocking cap. Over my socks and shoes I wore boots. The temperature went down to about freezing. By the end of the game it was almost impossible to walk. Several hours passed before normal circulation returned.

So here I was in the Methodist Church in Sidney. The speaker was retelling the story of her healing. It was a thrilling story. I was familiar with part of it. Genevieve (for she was the speaker) recounted stories of answered prayer. The service closed, and as people gathered to talk with Genevieve, we joined the group around her. Rather embarrassed, we told her that we had read her book, chatted a moment, and then turned away. To ask someone to pray for me was very difficult. It seemed like an imposition to take someone's time in this way. Disappointed we stood at the back of the church afraid to ask for prayer.

As we considered what to do, the church secretary came to us and asked if she could help. We explained our hesitation and trepidation. The secretary told us that Mrs. Parkhurst was very gracious and offered to tell her of our need. Soon we were in the pastor's study, which was quiet and peaceful. I explained my problem and my need and asked if she might pray for me. Without hesitation Genevieve consented.

The prayer flowed easily and I listened intently. Suddenly I heard "Amen" and I knew the prayer was ended. I was mortified because I felt I had fallen asleep. I heard only the beginning of the prayer and the very end. Genevieve told me later that I had just relaxed into the arms of Jesus. "Just lie down for a few minutes," she said. "This gives the healing power a chance to settle down through you." I rested for about an hour, dozing at times. Everything seemed so at peace. I seemed to be totally relaxed.

The day was cold and rainy. My wife and I had planned to go on and visit a friend about twenty-five miles away. As we drove, little was said about the prayer or how I felt. I remember saying that I was "tingling." At our destination I got out of the car and walked without stiffness. It seemed too good to be true.

As the days grew into weeks I became more and more sure that I had been healed. All the sleepiness left my hands immediately. I stopped taking the medicine. The index finger on my right hand which had begun to shrink in size began to look more normal. The blood flowed freely through my brain. Several weeks later I worked outside in sub-freezing weather, without gloves part of the time, with no more discomfort than any of the other men.

There were other indications that a healing had taken place which were almost more wonderful than the physical. My mind was much clearer. It was as though the fetters which had bound it were broken and my mind was set free. The Bible which had always seemed somewhat dull and uninteresting suddenly became alive and understandable.

This then was the result of God's power flowing through one of his channels for healing to bring honor and glory to the name of Jesus Christ.

Having said this, I must hasten to add that this is not the end of the story. This is only the end of chapter one. The final chapter is still a long way in the future. For me the healing began a great search.

Several weeks after I had been healed the psychologist in Tucson wrote to me, knowing nothing of the healing, and told me to purchase a book which had recently been published, *Prayer Can Change Your Life*.[1] She said she felt I was ready for this book. As I read it, I began to find how full of resentments I really was. With this realization came the knowledge that there was much that needed to be done in the way of spiritual growth.

After this healing there also came a great desire to help others in their search for wholeness, even as I had been helped. I had always felt an urging to be a minister but had never followed the leading. Even though I had been healed, it was very difficult to make a decision to go to college and get my training. I wanted to see the way clearly before I made the first step. We were expecting our fourth child and this did not help in overcoming what seemed to be insurmountable difficulties. The desire to help others increased. The urging toward the ministry grew stronger until finally in September, 1960, I took my entrance exams to begin my college work.

It was with a great deal of doubt that I decided to go to school. I was fearful I might not be admitted. I knew

---

[1] *Prayer Can Change Your Life,* Dr. William R. Parker and Elaine St. Johns, Prentice-Hall, Inc., Englewood Cliffs, N.J.

that at most there was money for only one year. I questioned if my children could ever go to school. I felt perhaps I was taking the schooling they should have. Would a man forty-three years old be able to learn?

I was admitted to college and began training in a special course which was to include some college and some seminary work. The course was to run for a minimum of two years, which seemed like a lifetime to me. Presently I am completing my seventh year of part-time study and expect to spend two or three more years in training.

The search, however, is not limited to an intellectual search through the college and seminary. Every year since my healing began with Genevieve's prayer, my family has taken out one or two weeks each year for intensive spiritual searching. If one wants to learn to weld, he consults a welding expert. If one wishes to learn spiritual truths, how to pray, how to become a channel for God's healing power, one consults experts in these fields and learns from them. Each vacation we spend some time in an attempt to learn from leaders like the Rev. and Mrs. Parkhurst, Dr. Frank Laubach, Mrs. Agnes Sanford, and others.

The seeds which were planted in Tucson began to grow into plants, and the seeking brought nourishment for the tender plants. Year by year as we searched the scriptures, read many wonderful books, listened to great lectures, growth came and a little fruit began to be produced. The progress was very slow but there was enough growth that we kept seeking.

In 1963 I was appointed as pastor of a small country church. Doors began to open, and I felt the desire to finish my college education. As the doors began to open wider, my wife also decided to get her college degree. My progress in school was rather slow, since I had an almost full time job at the college, working as a carpenter, besides my studies and the church. Two years after my appointment as pastor, since I had completed several years of non-credit seminary training and was studying for my degree at the college, the church of which I am a member graciously consented to ordain me since it is very difficult to carry on pastoral duties without ordination privileges. The ordination date was set for November 9th, just six years to the Sunday after the healing. One of the highlights of the day was to have Genevieve and George Parkhurst there.

The plants were being prepared so that God's life forces could flow more freely and more fruit was soon to be produced. We continued to set aside special periods of concentrated searching. During one of these times channels were opened and a new life seemed to fill us. Empowerment for action came even while we were still lay people.

One of the greatest parts of this healing story is the continuing expanding chain of lives that have been and are being changed. A great ministry appears to be opening for His glory. As I worked in the Ohio C.F.O. Camp God poured his healing power out to many. One of these people has kept in close contact and has consented to let me share his story with you.

At this Camp, Tom came to me saying that his heart was burdened and that he needed to talk. During one of the lectures he had become convinced that deeply buried in his subconscious was an almost forgotten incident which needed to be cleansed and forgiven. This experience dated back some twenty years. He also told me that for almost the same length of time he had suffered from hemorrhoids which were very painful. As we prayed together for forgiveness and cleansing for him, it suddenly occurred to me that with the spiritual cleansing complete there was also coming a physical healing. The physical healing came quickly. Most of his pain disappeared at once. In the year and a half that has intervened, the healing has been made perfect. Since Tom's healing he has been reaching out to help others through prayer as he was helped. So the chain lengthens.

Many other stories could be told. People are being healed and helped in almost every area of life. Emotional problems, suicide tendencies, malignancies, all respond to the power of God. Several months ago we began a healing service in our church in order to handle this expanding ministry while in college. Quietly God is blessing many who are seeking Him. Other ministers are holding evening healing services in their churches. Some conduct these in connection with the Sacrament of Holy Communion. They lay their hands on those who remain at the chancel after receiving the elements and pray for their healing. Such a service can be quiet and reverent, as persons who desire it wait, unhurried, in divine Presence.

Pastors once reluctant to attempt healing services, since as they say, they have no power to heal, yet as ordained ministers they have Jesus' commission to heal the sick, have found that in obedience to Him their lives and ministry have been blessed as they have allowed God's power to flow through them for the healing of others. Obedience to Christ brings His blessings.

XV

IN HIS LIVING PRESENCE

Genevieve Parkhurst:

It was a beautiful day in spring when the wife of an associate pastor of a sister church near my home came up the front walk to my door. I had met this gracious lady and admired her as she gave her talents and time to her church. Always assisting her husband and advancing his interests, she cheerfully worked in the background with children and youth, laboring quietly as she radiated sweetness like a violet in the shade.

She moved slowly as she approached the house, as if to enjoy the beauty of the morning. As we sat together she seemed hesitant to express what was on her heart. But this reticence only concealed a depth of character which was not revealed to many.

Here is her story exactly as she has written it.

Ruth Davis:

I was planning to have surgery as soon as the school year ended for our daughters. The condition of my gall bladder had been diagnosed as being twisted, perhaps from some childhood infection, and malfunctioning had gradually become worse. For more than six months it had been inflamed and I had not drawn a deep breath without pain that extended up under the right shoulder blade. The doctor had wanted to remove the gall bladder the previous December, but I had asked to put off the operation until summer, reasoning, how can you put a mother of young children in bed at Christmas time!

In the planning for carrying on responsibility at the church, I called a committee meeting before I left for the hospital. While we were waiting for all the members to arrive, one of the women mentioned Genevieve Parkhurst's book, *Healing and Wholeness are Yours,* and asked if any of us had read it. No one had and the conversation went on to other subjects and then the meeting began. Knowing what was ahead, the book's title intrigued me. I went to the nearby public library, found a copy, and checked it out. After I had finished reading the book, I so wanted to talk to Mrs. Parkhurst. My mind was full of questions. I had not believed that God worked in the world today in the way in which her book presented His power to heal. It did not occur to me to ask her to pray that I be healed without surgery. I felt that by talking over some of my questions there would surely be insights which would be helpful to my thinking.

I did not ask a single one of those questions but many of them have since been answered for me, experientially. When I confronted this poised, loving woman, all I said was, "I've just read your book and have come to talk with you. I'm leaving tomorrow to have gall bladder surgery." Before I could start on the questions in my mind, she asked some questions about my physical condition and began to talk to me of complete trust in God. "Would you like for me to pray for you?" she asked. I could not resist the sincerity and faith I encountered, and I found myself saying, "Would you?"

She knelt by the side of my chair and asked me to pray silently that I might trust God as completely as my children trusted me. Her quiet, simple, powerful prayer was directed to God for the healing of my body. At the close of her prayer she began quoting the 103rd Psalm and there was a vibration in her hands as she held them on my side and back. When this subsided and she rose, I breathed deeply and, from habit, started to tense my back to shield it from the pain deep breathing always caused, but no pain was there. I breathed deeply again and again, and still there was no pain. I sat quietly for some time before I could speak. "These are the first deep breaths I've taken in months without pain." I was so awed that I barely spoke in a whisper. She answered kindly, "I don't think you will need surgery."

At home that night, I prayed, "God, I don't understand what happened today, but just help me to trust you as completely as our young son trusts me."

During the night I woke up hearing music gloriously sung by an *a cappella* choir. It was "Christ we do all adore Thee and we do praise Thee forever," from DuBois' *The Seven Last Words of Christ*. With this music there was a light in the room, a light with a quality unlike any I had ever seen. In this light there was a presence, a loving, real presence as Christ appeared—not in physical presence as we know human form, but in radiant, glorious light and love. I felt a heat, very hot, in the area of my gall bladder, a deep penetrating heat accompanied by a strong pulling motion within, but there was no pain. When all was gone, I lay awake a long time. There was a calm over my whole being. I had been touched by the love of God and this love had truly cast out all fear. I was not even startled. It was as if this were the most natural of happenings. I was filled and surrounded by a peace that passed all understanding.

I went on to the hospital the next day. With the results of the tests which were run, my hospital stay ended. Instead of spending time recuperating from surgery, I visited in my mother's home where I had left the children. During this time I experienced a fellowship with the living Jesus which filled my heart until I felt it surely could contain no more. It was an adoration as expressed in the perfect harmony of the music the night He came with this most beautiful answer to my need.

With both my husband and Mrs. Parkhurst, I shared the experience as best I could express it. I recall her exact comment, "Bless you, my dear. Bless you all over"; and my joyous reply, "This is what has happened, this is exactly what has happened to me." I had been blessed much more than I knew.

For several years I had suffered with rheumatoid arthritis, which had been growing gradually worse. I found it very difficult to do my housework and care for our young son. Playing the piano or sewing for any length of time left my hands numb. Using my arms and shoulders left the back of my neck tight and often my tongue was also numb. My feet were comfortable only in low-heeled shoes. Although it had become an effort to even get out of bed in the mornings, something did not let me give up. I was afraid to stop being active lest I become unable to do the things I knew had to be done to keep a household running. I took hot baths and exercises to get my body moving for the day.

Knowing the reality of the Presence of Jesus and that my gall bladder was healed seemed more than I could ask and certainly more than I could comprehend. I did not even think of asking for further healing.

I was in the church one Saturday afternoon in late June practicing the organ for the Sunday worship service, as the organist was on vacation. One of the hymns selected for use was "Spirit of God, Descent Upon My Heart." The words became my prayer as I played:

> I ask no dream, no prophet ecstacy,
> no sudden rending of the veil of clay,
> no heavenly visitant no opening skies . . .

My mind and heart were full. "O God, it's not that we ask for any of these, but, by your Grace, at times they're sent." With the words "But take the dimness of my soul away," my prayer continued, "O God, this is all I ask. Take the dimness of my soul away." And then I heard a voice and thinking someone had come into the sanctuary I stopped playing. I immediately realized there was no one present and that the voice was above me. It was saying as it moved toward the back of the sanctuary where there is a window with the symbolic lamb in its center: "This is your prayer's answer. This has been done for you. Behold the lamb of God that taketh away the sin of the world." I stood in the presence of such power. Something then came down over me, over my head first, and then through my whole body. It was warm, powerful, and penetrating. I don't know how long I stood there. As I walked out of the building into the late afternoon, colors and sounds seemed so very distinct. It was as if all my senses had been keenly sharpened, and I wished for time to just continue walking.

During that night I perspired heavily. The next morning the stiffness in the joints of my body was greatly relieved. I felt physically exhausted from the perspiring, but my spirit mounted to the very heavens that day as I worshipped in the church. As I played the hymn, "Spirit of God," I wept with gratitude and joy. During the weeks that followed, I awoke every morning feeling a deep, rhythmic, flowing warmth, sometimes with a gentle vibrating quality, flowing through my body, and with it came healing. This continued until October 1st, when healing was complete.

My husband and I went to the Parkhursts' home to share the further healing experience that was taking place as the arthritis left my body. I remember the note of joyous thanksgiving in the prayers of the Rev. and Mrs. Parkhurst, and my husband and that I could find no words to express what I felt that night as the four of us joined hands in a circle of prayer. As we were leaving, Mrs. Parkhurst suggested that I treat myself to the luxury of rest as if I had had surgery for I had had divine surgery. During those summer and early fall months I spent many hours in quiet rest, in which I was held so close in divine love and yet at the same time was flung to heights I had not dreamed existed.

Truly, "the word of God is alive and active" (Heb. 4:12). God used Mrs. Parkhurst as His channel to open to me the doors of the Kingdom of God on earth. I heard harmonies from Heaven. I heard the voice and experienced the ministry of the Spirit of the Living God—living and present with me. I saw the light of the Presence of the Son of God. I felt the warmth of the love of God through my entire being. I was lifted above my body to the lightness and pure joy of divine freedom. Surely to die to this life must be to gain this relationship eternally. But, how much of the blessed relationship is ours now if we can only trust God completely to provide every good and perfect gift for us. To know Him aright is surely to grow in living this eternal life now. This is my quest. God grant me guidance toward this goal.

Genevieve Parkhurst:

Persons who seek God only for physical healing are not likely to be greatly benefited even though they may be healed physically, while the lives of others may be greatly enriched through suffering as they seek spiritual development through their prayers for healing. Suffering can be a blessing, when through it the power of God is so revealed that thereafter there can be no doubt as to His power and goodness.

More than two years before Mrs. Davis' healing experience, she and her husband received an inquiry from their Mission Board as to their availability for missionary service. At that time she did not consider her illness a barrier to such service and they answered, expressing willingness to serve in this area. However, there was no response from the Mission Board, and they dismissed the matter.

More than a year later, a letter from the Mission Board arrived, stating their reply to the letter of inquiry had been misplaced in a file drawer, and had been recovered in the process of changing office secretaries. At that time the arthritis had so advanced that missionary service seemed a remote possibility. But God touched Mrs. Davis and healing took place. Something like nine months passed in which no symptoms of the illness returned. The Davises then made formal application and all medical and psychological tests were passed. Today they are serving their Church in Mexico.

Paul said, "He that cometh to God must believe that he is, and that he is a rewarder of them that diligently seek him" (Heb. 11:6). Today, as Mrs. Davis works among people who look to her for instruction, she can speak with certainty, for her belief in God has risen to knowledge of Him. She speaks with authority when she says that He is a rewarder of them that diligently seek Him.

Surely, "all things work together for good to them that love God, to them who are called according to his purpose."

XVI

THIS TREASURE IN EARTHEN VESSELS

H E WHO IS BLESSED by Divine Spirit is endowed with a priceless treasure. The treasure is greater than the vessel which contains it, yet this only magnifies the greatness of the treasure. Saint Paul says in Second Corinthians (4:7): "We have this treasure in earthen vessels, that the excellency of the power may be of God, and not of us."

Perhaps we are privileged to receive such divine excellency because we are citizens of two worlds. Our spirits are of our Father in Heaven, but our bodies are clay of Mother Earth. Yet, we need not despise this clay, rather we should glorify it. Is it not the excellency of God's Spirit indwelling our bodies that enables them to be "temples of the Holy Spirit"?

God seems to love variety. Human bodies differ in capacity, size, shape, and color. Yet, whether they are tall or short, graceful or sturdy, each has its own charm and uniqueness. Our earthen vessels have varied colorings, also. They may be pale and delicate, yellow, or brown, or a glossy black. Like the ceramic vase, our coloring, once placed in the firing, cannot be changed. The genes which determine our physical characteristics are bequeathed to us by our forebears, and, accepting them wisely, we can use them to advantage.

A teenage girl, sensitive of her appearance, was wailing because she was taller and heavier than her companions. Her grandfather, a large man who had spent his life on a cattle ranch, put his arm around her and smilingly said, "Kitten, could you expect a Shetland pony from a strain of Clydesdales?"

The girl raised her head and retorted, "A tall man with broad shoulders and a deep chest is a fine specimen of manhood, but when his daughter is built the same way, it is hard to take."

Kindly, the elderly gentleman replied, "Since your body is God's temple, be a cathedral for God."

The granddaughter studied the benevolent face she had taken for granted all the years of her ilfe. Her eyes lighted as the truth he exemplified dawned upon her.

"Who would have thought of that but you, Grandaddy? A cathedral for God. That is something to live up to."

Youth often is dissatisfied with the endowments Nature has given them. Most young men wish to be tall and strong while girls prefer a petite figure. Yet, most persons attain their place in life through the development of their intelligence and agreeable co-operation with others. Many men whose heads have not towered above their fellows have achieved enviable places of leadership through hard work and an outgoing personality.

It is natural that every girl wants to be beautiful. It is wise to accentuate our good qualities and minimize the worst, but it is better to make the most of all our natural endowments and forget our defects. She who is in good health, carries herself proudly, talks easily, and listens to others with interest, is kind to persons of all ages, need not be beautiful. She will be loved.

Sometimes misfortune hinders an individual's normal development, yet, as the years pass, it becomes evident that his life has been turned into channels of greater activity and satisfaction than he otherwise might have known.

The little Negro boy called George Washington Carver suffered from whooping cough so that his frailty made him unable to work as other boys did. He was allowed to wander in the woods and upon sunny hills where he made companions of flowers. He talked to them and listened for their messages to him. After he became a great scientist, it was his custom to go into the woods at four o'clock each morning and there ask, "Mister Creator, what have you to teach me today?" Thirsting for knowledge, he once asked Mister Creator to tell him the purpose of the universe. The answer came to him, "This question is too great for your mind. Ask something your size." Humbly he asked that he might understand the value of the peanut. So it was that Dr. Carver discovered over two hundred uses for the lowly peanut and nearly as many for the sweet potato.

Thomas A. Edison suffered a defect of hearing in his early boyhood, said to have resulted from a slap on his ears. This misfortune was at least partially responsible for the poor school work which caused him to be expelled. It has been said, that spared the regimentation of years of schooling and permitted him to learn truths from the wisdom within himself and from above. No doubt his deafness enabled him to shut out the distractions about him and concentrate on the hundreds of inventions he gave to the world. He himself said he did not make these inventions, but that they came through him.

The vessels in which our spirits dwell may become marred or misshapen. Still, the divine treasure often glows within them with a radiant light. One of the most admirable men I ever have known carried a dark red-brown birthmark over all one side of his face. No doubt he suffered much when a boy because of this disfiguration, but he rose to such heights of character that all who knew him admired and respected him. He, like many others, was a living witness to the truth that the "excellency of the treasure" is not lessened by the vessel in which it is held.

A remarkable person, whom I am proud to call my friend, lost a leg when she was a girl. For sixty years this vibrant lady has walked on an artificial limb. She has done the work of two women and has accomplished more than most women with two good legs ever do. The vessel, though chipped, can be beautiful as the spirit within is radiant.

Another friend lost one hand in an accident. Yet she does her housework efficiently and gives her lovely voice in song. Audiences are inspired by her singing, and those who do not know her never suspect that the stub of one arm is concealed in the folds of her skirt or behind her back as she pours out her joy of living in music.

A man who must go on crutches or in a wheel chair as the result of polio suffered when a child is a living witness to the excellency of the spirit within. His mind is strong, his attitudes wholesome, and his outlook on life optimistic. By comparison, he puts many with strong bodies to shame.

As often is the case, God seems to compensate those who must endure some loss with an overabundance of His sustaining grace.

There has been much speculation as to what Saint Paul's "thorn in the flesh" might have been. Paul says of it, "Lest I should be exalted above measure through the abundance of the revelations, there was given to me a thorn in the flesh, the messenger of Satan to buffet me . . ." (II Cor. 12:7).

This "thorn" could have been exactly what he said it was, an evil influence that sought to hinder his ministry. Possibly it was persons who were envious of him, or some who were resentful that he left them to follow Christ. Or, as he said, this thorn may have been some condition which kept him humble. God did pour through the Apostle Paul an abundance of the revelations of His will, His purpose, and His glory. Paul, being conscious of his human weakness, may have felt God was gracious in giving him some weight on the wings of his spirit in order to keep his feet on the ground.

There can be blessings in adversity. Because of some physical imperfection many persons have turned to spiritual powers for the fulfillment of their lives. Here is a great truth. When a thing which is close to a person's heart is given to God, that person seems to be blessed in abundant measure. It is natural that an individual feels resentful toward whatever caused his injury. Resentment creates strong emotion. When strong emotional stress is released, it seems to create a vortex, into which God's love and abundant grace may flow to fill the empty space.

Jesus gave His highest commendations to persons who gave that which was most dear to them to Him and His kingdom. A woman gave two coins, which was all her money; Mary of Magdela gave all her adoration; a woman sensitive that her race was called dogs gave all her pride; Mary of Bethany gave all her devotion; a Roman Centurion gave all his trust; Peter gave all his loyalty; and Paul gave all his fervor and his keen mind with its educational training in service of Christ. All of these persons were blessed by Him and were happy in His reward.

The excellency of divine treasure makes any life more valuable and sometimes it seems to glow most brightly in vessels that are slightly marred by some imperfection.

This life is a time for becoming. None is perfect, yet all are given opportunity for growth. Adversities may seem to slow our progress, yet difficulties can call forth our determination to overcome them. Through overcoming we find we have grown stronger. Confusion may confound us, but God is not the author of confusion.

Good, not evil comes from God. God is love, mercy, and creative good. He is the author of peace, the giver of light and life. His will is for His childrens' good, from the least to the greatest, whatever they may have to endure—"Even so it is not the will of your Father which is in heaven, that one of these little ones should perish" (Matt. 18:14). Mental health is our Father's will for us—"For God hath not given us the spirit of fear; but of power, and of love, and of a sound mind" (II Tim. 1:7). God wishes us to have physical health and prosperity—"Beloved, I wish above all things that thou mayest prosper and be in health, even as thy soul prospereth" (III Jn. 2). God's will for us is wholeness in every area of life.

He meets us where we are when we turn to Him in sincerity, seeking Him with all our hearts. We fail when we try to use God to further our own plans. Such effort may produce much of the confusion and frustration we suffer.

When we allow God to be supreme in our lives and harmonize our thoughts, desires, and actions with His, then He gives us His Spirit to strengthen our weakness. In God there is balm for healing, yes, even for HEALING THE WHOLE PERSON.

* * * * *

POSTSCRIPT

I regret that it is not possible for me to write to persons who may send letters to me asking for prayer for themselves or others. I am not wise enough to answer questions or give advice, but I shall join in prayer with anyone who will release their request to the Father (as I shall do when praying for them) and who will believe that I am praying for them even though they do not receive a letter saying I am doing so.

There are consecrated persons who will pray and answer letters.

THE UNITED PRAYER TOWER, which is associated with the Camps Farthest Out, exists for the purpose of praying for persons who contact them. On the back of their monthly publication, *The Prayer Manual,* is this invitation: "If you have requested help from the United Prayer Tower, someone, somewhere, is in prayer for you. With the time changing around the world, members of the Prayer Tower family are lifting YOU to God in love and prayer around the clock. Remember this! YOU ARE NEVER ALONE." Their address:

The United Prayer Tower, 3900 10th Avenue, Minneapolis, Minnesota 55407. Telephone: 822-5544.

THE ABUNDANT LIFE PRAYER GROUP at Oral Roberts University, Tulsa, Oklahoma, exists for the purpose of helping people in need of prayer. Twenty-four hours a day, seven days a week, prayer partners are on duty in the Prayer Tower, praying and counseling on the telephone. Each call is answered by a dedicated and trained Christian counselor. For prayer, day or night, call RI 3-7971 (Area Code 918), Tulsa, Oklahoma, or write The Abundant Life Prayer Group, Oral Roberts University, 7777 South Lewis, Tulsa, Oklahoma 74105.

Magazines on Christian healing, which also list churches where healing services are held:

Sharing—an International Journal of Christian Healing, Order of St. Luke the Physician, 2243 Front St., San Diego, California 92102.

He Is Able—dedicated to restoring healing in the Methodist Church, 814 Broad St., Chattanooga, Tennessee 73402.